You are already making meaning.

This book reveals its shape.

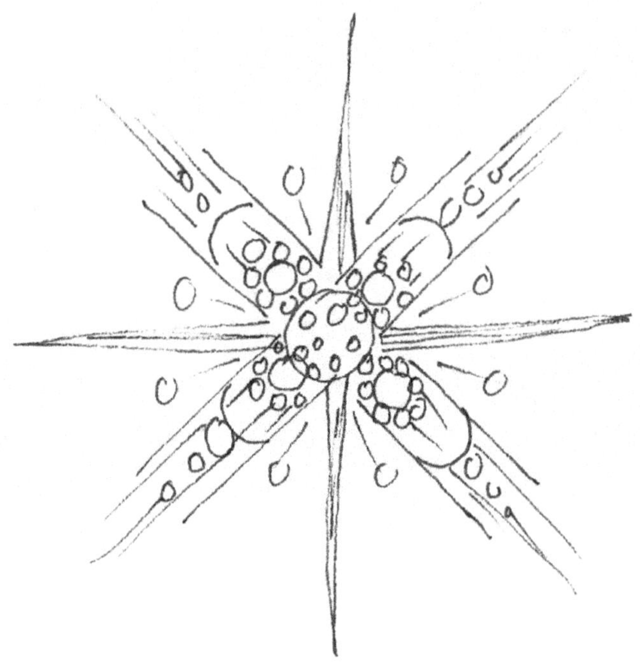

# You Know More Than You Think
## A Five-Book Series

Book Three
## The Shape of Knowing
Explorations in the Landscape of Meaning

### Elly Flippen

A BIOMIND SUPERPOWERS BOOK
PUBLISHED BY

Swann-Ryder Productions, LLC

## DISCLAIMER

This book is provided for informational, educational, and experiential purposes only. It is not intended as medical, psychological, psychiatric, therapeutic, legal, or scientific advice, nor should it be used as a substitute for professional diagnosis, treatment, or consultation.

The author is affiliated with Swann-Ryder Productions, LLC, which holds certain copyrights and related intellectual property rights to the published and unpublished writings and artwork of Ingo Swann. This book may reference, quote, or discuss his published material for educational and contextual purposes. All interpretations, analyses, applications, and contemporary extensions presented herein are solely those of the author.

Nothing in this book should be interpreted as representing official positions of any scientific, governmental, institutional, or research organization. References to perception research, anomalous experience, or non-ordinary awareness are included for historical, educational, and phenomenological exploration.

This work does not claim to prove, validate, or guarantee the existence of paranormal, psychic, extrasensory, or supernatural abilities, nor does it present such phenomena as scientifically established fact.

Individual experiences will vary. No guarantees are made regarding outcomes, results, insights, or personal transformation.

Readers are responsible for their own engagement with the material and for their physical, emotional, and psychological well-being. Individuals with a history of trauma, dissociation, significant mental health conditions, neurological or cardiovascular concerns, or other medical conditions should consult a qualified healthcare professional before engaging in any practices described.

The practices described in this book are voluntary exercises intended for personal exploration and should be approached with discretion and self-awareness.

While reasonable efforts have been made to ensure the accuracy of the information presented, the author and Swann-Ryder Productions, LLC assume no responsibility for errors or omissions and make no warranties regarding the completeness, reliability, or applicability of the material.

By choosing to engage with this book, the reader accepts responsibility for its use and for any decisions or actions arising from the material presented.

**READER GUIDANCE**

The following guidance is offered to support safe, grounded, and thoughtful engagement with the practices and explorations presented in this book.

Readers are encouraged to:

- Move at a pace that feels appropriate and sustainable.
- Modify, pause, or discontinue any practice that creates discomfort, distress, or instability.
- Seek qualified professional support when encountering intense emotional, psychological, or perceptual experiences.

The material in this book is not intended to replace sound judgment, professional care, or responsible engagement with daily life, relationships, and decision-making.

These practices are offered as invitations to explore awareness and perceptual literacy, not as doctrines of belief, systems of authority, or substitutes for medical, psychological, or therapeutic care.

Your consent, grounding, safety, and discernment are foundational to your engagement with the material presented here.

# TABLE OF CONTENTS

# HOW TO APPROACH THIS BOOK

This volume continues the exploration begun in the previous books. It is not material to master, but material to move through with attention.

Understanding develops here through recognition rather than explanation. If grounding, regulation, and boundary stability have begun to stabilize, you may notice that what appears consciously often emerges earlier in the process, before it becomes emotion, narrative, or conclusion. This book explores that earlier organization.

Some sections may register immediately; others may remain indistinct at first. This is natural. Your organismic intelligence differentiates gradually as familiarity deepens.

The pages that follow are designed to orient attention. If something does not come into focus right away, allow it to remain unforced. Recognition often emerges through lived engagement rather than effort.

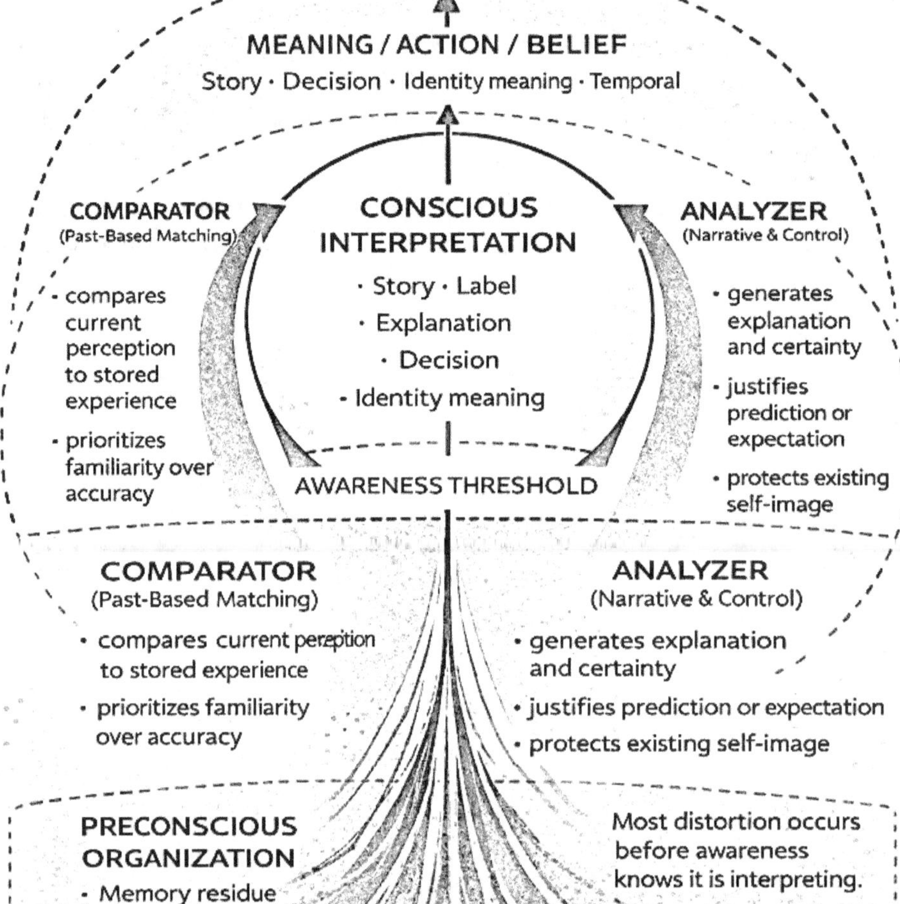


MEANING / ACTION / BELIEF
Story · Decision · Identity meaning · Temporal

COMPARATOR
(Past-Based Matching)
· compares current perception to stored experience
· prioritizes familiarity over accuracy

CONSCIOUS INTERPRETATION
· Story · Label
· Explanation
· Decision
· Identity meaning

ANALYZER
(Narrative & Control)
· generates explanation and certainty
· justifies prediction or expectation
· protects existing self-image

AWARENESS THRESHOLD

COMPARATOR
(Past-Based Matching)
· compares current perception to stored experience
· prioritizes familiarity over accuracy

ANALYZER
(Narrative & Control)
· generates explanation and certainty
· justifies prediction or expectation
· protects existing self-image

PRECONSCIOUS ORGANIZATION
· Memory residue
· Conditioning

Most distortion occurs before awareness knows it is interpreting.

RAW PERCEPTUAL SIGNAL
(somatic · emotional · relational · symbolic · temporal)

## The Diagram

The preceding diagram is not meant to be analyzed in advance. It serves as a reference for dynamics that become observable through experience:

> how information organizes before interpretation
> how emotional tone and attentional bias shape meaning
> how organization supports discernment
> how urgency and overload introduce distortion
> how boundaries stabilize meaning without constricting it

Recognition may come later, often when a shift in intensity occurs without an obvious external cause. When that happens, return to the diagram.

It is a pattern to recognize as organization shifts, not a problem to solve.

This book does not seek to eliminate meaning-making. It clarifies how meaning forms, where it stabilizes naturally, and where distortion enters so that information becomes more differentiated, and more trustworthy over time.


## Reading as Experience

This book works through accumulation and cross-reference rather than linear explanation.

Each chapter introduces distinctions that may feel partial on their own but clarify as patterns recur across contexts. Recognition often arrives retrospectively: in daily life rather than during structured exploration.

The term *layer* is used throughout to describe different modes of organization. In lived experience these are not stacked levels but interdependent processes occurring simultaneously within the same system.

The explorations are not techniques to perform correctly. They are structured opportunities to observe how meaning is shaped in real time.

If effort increases, pause. Discrimination sharpens through steadiness rather than force.

Nothing new is being introduced. Earlier stages of organization are simply becoming observable.


## Pace, Repetition, & Sequence

A steady rhythm (for example, one chapter per week) allows sufficient time for integration. Speed offers no advantage.

Chapters may be entered non-sequentially if necessary, but the material gains depth when encountered in continuity.

The perceptual-awareness interchange process does not move in a straight line.

What feels indistinct may later become obvious; what feels clear may later differentiate further.

Repetition does not reproduce experience; it refines discrimination.

With recurrence, earlier stages of organization become easier to detect before they consolidate into reaction.

Consistency matters more than intensity.

Familiarity builds reliability.

# GETTING READY

Before beginning these explorations, pause to consider how meaning is approached in this volume and how attention is steadied as it takes form.

This is not a list of cautions, but an orientation to the ground from which the material unfolds.

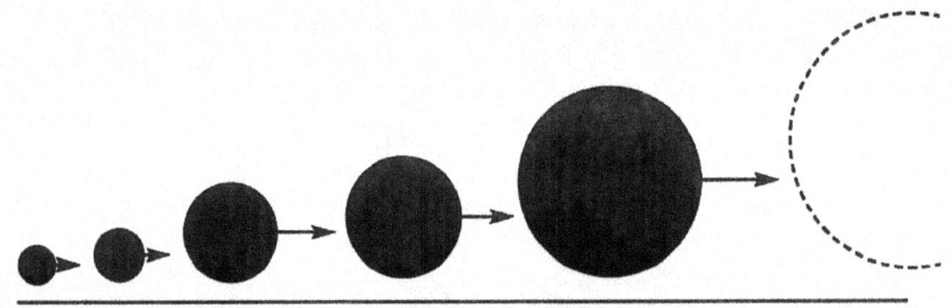


DEVELOPMENT

## Approaching the Explorations

This book is not a belief system. Nothing here requires adopting metaphysical claims or accepting ideas on authority. You are asked only to notice experience and develop discernment around how meaning forms.

What you perceive does not become accurate because it feels meaningful. Meaning does not become reliable because it feels vivid. Recognition matters more than belief. Discernment matters more than interpretation. If something does not land, leave it. The process clarifies through direct engagement.

The explorations that follow are temporary orientations, not states to maintain. They are designed to help you notice specific dynamics. Once an exploration concludes, allow your system to return to its natural baseline.

As what you notice becomes subtler, remain close to direct sensation. Images, impressions, or fleeting associations may arise, but there is no need to interpret them immediately. Information often registers first as tone or bodily sensation before meaning becomes explicit.

Each exploration also includes *What to Watch For* and reflection questions.

> *What to Watch For* points are not predictions or guarantees. They are orientation cues, examples of how shifts may appear, so they are less likely to be overlooked.
> *Reflection* questions are not meant to be answered correctly. They are invitations to remain with your experience long enough for it to clarify. If other questions arise, you are encouraged to follow them as well.

From this point forward, however, the explanatory sections used earlier in the series (such as the *Why This Happens* reflections) no longer appear.

At this stage, explanation becomes less useful than observation. The emphasis shifts toward noticing how perceptual information organizes within your own experience before interpretation is added.

Each person's perceptual system is different. Rather than supplying interpretations in advance, this book (and the two that follow) invites you to observe how meaning forms as your experience unfolds.

If something feels charged, accelerated, or diffuse, return to what is directly felt. Allow sensation to anchor your attention before attempting to understand what is occurring.

If intensity rises or clarity drops, pause and reestablish orientation:

> breath
> posture
> engagement with physical sensation
> awareness of the room
> ordinary spatial orientation

All differentiation depends on stability. Earlier phases of organization become observable only when your system remains steady.

Brief resets (breath regulation, boundary stabilization, and perceptual reorientation) remain available throughout this work.

They are not corrective measures, but regulatory supports.

Additional exercises that support grounding and perceptual reset are included in the Appendix and may be returned to whenever steadiness needs to be reestablished.


## Reflection Spaces

Throughout the book you will encounter pauses:

> Pause. Check resonance.
> Notice what you're noticing.

These are not prompts to analyze. They are spaces where what you notice can settle and take shape without interference.

What you perceive may arrive:

> before words
> before emotion settles
> before meaning organizes
> as symbol, pattern, or early recognition

Throughout the book you will also find spaces where reflections can land. These are not assignments to complete. They are simply places where perception can pause long enough to register.

Sometimes this may appear as a word or short phrase.

Sometimes it may appear as a simple mark, a line, or a quick sketch.

Drawing, diagramming, or loosely tracing shapes can allow early impressions to organize without forcing them into explanation.

Nothing needs to be captured precisely. A few marks, a brief note, or nothing at all is sufficient. Silence is a valid response.

Perceptual coherence does not come from capturing experience. It comes from allowing it.

Let the process unfold.

Let meaning follow.

**Key Takeaway**

There is always more occurring in organismic perception than what reaches passive awareness. Subtle signals often arise before thought intervenes.

As active awareness expands while remaining grounded, information becomes more distinct and more dependable.

This book helps you recognize how meaning forms so clarity can deepen without distortion.

What follows is not something to get right.

It is an invitation to explore the landscape of meaning.

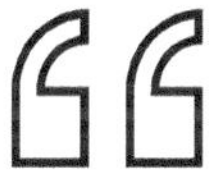

Often, subtle perceptual signals register within the body before they reach conscious awareness.

The system responds (through unease, tension, or a quiet sense of apprehension) without yet knowing why.

Only later does understanding catch up, when external events reveal what the body had already begun to register.

— Adapted from Ingo Swann, *Everybody's Guide to Natural ESP*

# THE LANDSCAPE OF MEANING

# THE DEEPER ARCHITECTURE OF ORGANISMIC INTELLIGENCE

**A Necessary Pause Before Going Deeper**

You've already done something essential.

In Book One, you explored how to notice.

In Book Two, you navigated through how to stabilize what you notice.

Because of that foundation, what you take in can now deepen without becoming confusing or overwhelming.

Before it does, however, there is one structure that must be made explicit: it is not as a technique, but as the underlying organization through which your organismic intelligence already operates.

As noted in Book One, Ingo observed that information never enters a neutral system. It arrives within a system shaped by experience, emotion, habit, culture, and belief.

Perception and awareness do not simply "turn on."

They reorganizes.

This book explores that reorganization.

The diagrams and explanations that follow are not theories to adopt.

They are orientation tools, methods for making visible how incoming information is organized before it becomes conscious interpretation.

Seeing this process allows your organismic perception and active awareness to function with greater discrimination between signal and response, and with reduced interference from prior narrative, emotional charge, or attentional narrowing.

# THE ORGANIZATION OF PERCEPTION

## CONSCIOUS AWARENESS

*Thoughts, images, and interpretations*

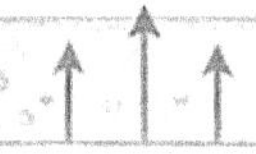

## CULTURAL & PERSONAL FRAMEWORKS

*What is trusted, ignored, or dismissed*

Education · Belief systems · Language · Social norms · identity roles

## MIND-MAP

*Habitual patterns that translate sensation into meaning*

Attention habits · Memory · Association · Emotional weighing

## REGULATION & COHERENCE

*Breath, posture, and nervous system balance determine signal stability*

Breath rhythm · Muscle tone · Emotional load · Coherence

## ORGANISMIC SENSING

*Continuous bodily, emotional, and relational registration*
(always active, often unnoticed)

*Perception does not fail because signal is absent.*
*It falters when signal is obscured by interference.*

**The Shape of Meaning**

What you notice, name, or understand is the end of a process, not the beginning.

The perceptual–awareness interchange process starts much earlier, at the level of bodily sensing, emotional tone, and nervous-system regulation.

From there, information moves through internal organization before it ever appears as a thought, image, or conclusion.

Meaning does not appear fully formed. It is assembled as information moves through your system. In simplified form, the process looks like this:

〉 **Organismic sensing.**
Your body continuously detects internal state, relational presence, and environmental change. This ongoing detection is the signal: raw data before interpretation. It is always active, whether noticed or not.

〉 **Regulatory conditions.**
Breath, posture, emotional load, perceptual coherence, and boundaries determine how clearly that signal can move forward without fragmenting or distorting.

〉 **The mind-map.**
Habitual patterns of attention, memory, and association translate raw sensation into recognizable form.

〉 **The reality framework.**
Learned assumptions determine what information is trusted, dismissed, or explained away.

Only after moving through these stages does what is detected become something you are consciously aware of, appearing as language, images, symbols, or understanding.

Nothing is added or removed in this process. What changes is the signal-to-noise ratio: the balance between what is actually being detected and the interference introduced by stress, projection, premature interpretation, or assumption.

Clarity does not come from amplifying what you recognize. It comes from reducing interference, rebalancing what is signal and what is noise.

Often the first step is simply noticing what repeats before deciding what it means.

## Why Your Mind-Map Feels Like Reality

The internal map you live inside feels complete because it is the only version of reality you encounter directly.

> Your perceptual awareness system samples.
> Your attention selects.
> Your intellect organizes.

The result is a coherent, navigable world that feels like "what is," even though it is a construction: a usable model rather than total reality.

This is not a flaw. It is how the process works.

If you were to register everything at once (every sound, every micro-shift, every relational cue) you would be overwhelmed. So, your system filters, compresses, and simplifies.

This is why:

> background noise disappears until relevance appears
> emotional tone becomes obvious only after attunement
> meaning often seems to arrive fully formed rather than gradually

As regulation improves, your map changes. It does not replace what you notice; it allows more to register.

Patterns stand out sooner.

Direction becomes perceptible before outcome.

Information that would overwhelm literal perception arrives in compressed form.

This is not imagination filling gaps.

It is your system organizing more information than can be processed linearly.

# Getting Out of the Box
# Requires Understanding the Box

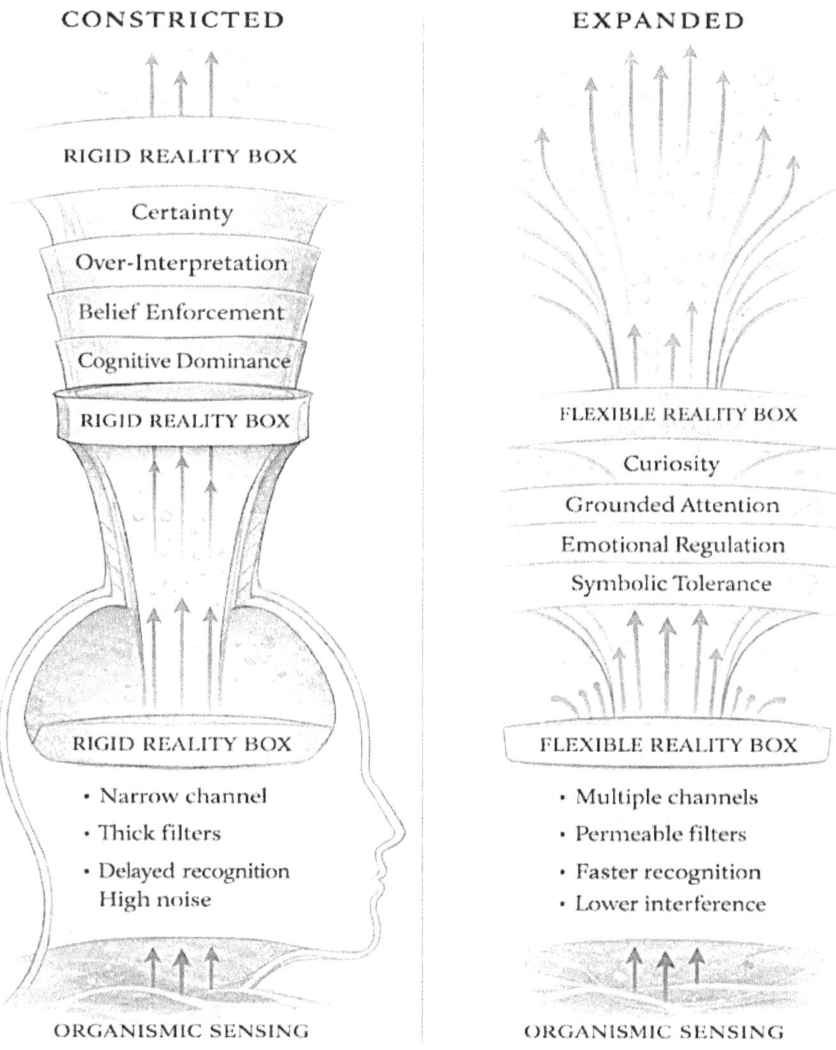



*The reality box is an artifact within the mind.*
*Perception expands not by escaping structure, but by*
*restoring flexibility to it.*

## Understanding the Box Before Moving Beyond It

A reality box is not reality itself. It is the intellect's organizing structure: a patterned set of assumptions, attentional habits, and learned frames through which experience is encountered.

"Getting out of the box" is often imagined as escape.

But escape is not the right metaphor.

The diagram illustrates two versions of the same structure: one constricted, one flexible. In both cases organismic sensing feeds upward. What changes is not the presence of structure, but how it filters and organizes what passes through it.

The broader social and cultural structures that shape mind-maps and reality frameworks are explored more fully in Book Five. Here, the focus remains on recognizing how meaning organizes within your own perceptual system.

A rigid reality box:

> narrows channels and thickens filters
> reinforces certainty through interpretation and belief defense
> reduces variability
> slows recognition and increases interference
> filters out what does not fit before it fully registers

A flexible reality box does not abandon structure. It restores permeability.

A flexible reality box:

> keeps multiple channels available
> replaces certainty with curiosity
> uses emotional regulation to stabilize attention
> allows faster recognition because less energy is spent defending a single frame

The most limiting aspect of a reality box is often not what it contains, but what never reaches awareness because it is filtered too early.

You do not have one fixed map.

You have a system capable of holding many.

Knowing this does not eliminate structure. It restores flexibility.

As flexibility increases, what you notice does not become louder.

It becomes more efficient: fewer distortions, less noise, faster recognition.

## Final Orientation: Symbols

In Books One and Two, experience was anchored through concrete reference points:

> breath
> posture
> boundary
> emotional regulation

In this volume, information may be noticed earlier, before those anchors are obvious. It may appear as impressions, recurring patterns, symbolic fragments, or understated recognitions rather than explicit conclusions.

This does not mean experience is becoming vague or imagined. It means your system is registering patterns before they have consolidated into explanation or language.

Some of what emerges in this territory may resemble what Carl Jung called archetypes: recurring patterns of meaning that appear across cultures and historical periods.

Jung described archetypes not as inherited images, but as inherited potentials: organizing structures within the psyche (the domain in which perception, feeling, memory, and meaning arise and interact) that shape how certain themes, roles, and relational dynamics take form.

Across time, these patterns appear in different clothing:

> The Initiate appears as the immigrant, new parent, graduate, or patient receiving a diagnosis.
> The Orphan / Exile appears as the outsider, transfer student, refugee, whistleblower, or anyone navigating belonging from the edge of a group.
> The Seeker appears as the student, researcher, explorer, pilgrim, or anyone driven by the search for understanding.
> The Fool / Beginner appears as the newcomer, apprentice, disruptive learner, or the person willing to risk embarrassment in order to discover something new.
> The Creator / Builder appears as the artist, engineer, entrepreneur, designer, researcher, or anyone shaping something that did not previously exist.
> The Caretaker becomes the over-functioning parent, burnout professional, or friend who absorbs tension.
> The Guardian appears as the protector, regulator, moderator, security figure, or person responsible for maintaining safety, order, or boundaries.

> The Mediator appears as the negotiator, therapist, diplomat, conflict resolver, or family member translating tension between opposing sides.
> The Authority shows up as a judge, CEO, institution, or algorithmic voice.
> The Rebel emerges as an activist, whistleblower, cultural critic, or adolescent pushing against constraint.
> The Trickster appears as the satirist, meme-creator, hacker, comedian, or disruptive innovator.
> The Scapegoat appears in family systems, workplaces, and online communities.
> The Hero's Descent shows up as addiction and recovery, public failure, divorce, career collapse, and reinvention.
> The Destroyer / Transformer appears as crisis, illness, revolution, restructuring, or any force that dismantles what no longer holds.
> The Shadow appears as disowned traits projected outward or qualities that surface under stress.
> The Witness appears as the journalist, historian, documentarian, observer, or quiet participant who notices and records what others overlook.
> The Wise Elder becomes the therapist, seasoned mentor, experienced leader, or trusted grandparent.

Rather than stereotypes or rigid roles, these patterns describe recurring ways experience begins to organize before personal narrative fully forms.

They do not dictate behavior.

They shape perception.

They influence what feels significant, threatening, magnetic, or meaningful before explanation catches up.

In this book, archetypes are approached not as mythic abstractions, but as observable patterns in how meaning organizes itself.

When such patterns arise, the task is not to decide what they mean, but to slow down and notice what is taking shape.

Awareness often precedes explanation. And sometimes, just being aware is enough.

What follows is not an entry into something unusual.

It is a quieter encounter with patterns that have always participated in shaping experience.

As what you perceive begins registering these deeper organizing patterns, information often appears in symbolic form rather than as direct explanation

## Why Symbol Appears as Perception Deepens

As what you recognize enlarges beyond your literal channels, information often arrives compressed.

When bodily sensing, emotional tone, spatial awareness, relational context, and pattern recognition shows up simultaneously, your organismic intelligence needs an efficient format.

Symbol is one such format.

Symbols are not fantasy.

They are dense packets of meaning.

A symbol can carry:

> pattern without explanation
> relationship without narrative
> direction without conclusion

This is why symbolic perception increases as what you become aware of becomes more active rather than conceptual. Your system is processing more information at once, not less.

Symbol does not mean imaginary. It means efficient instead.

Because symbolic perception compresses meaning, learning to work with symbols becomes an important form of perceptual literacy


## Why Symbolic Literacy Matters

Without symbolic literacy, your organismic intelligence's process often breaks down in predictable ways:

1. Over-literalizing symbols.
2. Dismissing subtle information.
3. Forcing meaning too quickly.
4. Inflating perception into certainty or identity.

Symbolic literacy allows your system's processes to deepen without losing grounding. It keeps your awareness flexible, embodied, and discerning rather than rigid or dogmatic.

*Pause. Check resonance.*

# 12 | The Deep Background
## Where Perception Extends

### Opening Invitation

Up to this point, you've been navigating through noticing:

- your own perceptual space
- the area around your body
- the atmosphere of rooms
- the presence of other people
- emotional tone influences within and around you

These are essential capacities. They form the foreground of organismic perception: what is most immediate and easiest to notice.

Beneath this foreground is something broader and less reactive.

A background of awareness that organizes information before interpretation appears.

You may recognize it when:

- you enter a place and sense its history
- you know what someone will say before they speak
- a shift registers before events unfold
- a room's mood is clear before interaction
- awareness comes to rest in a deep, spacious quiet
- knowing arrives as movement rather than thought
- what you are aware of extends beyond the immediate moment

This is what we'll call the deep background.

It is not a separate place or state. It is the background orientation against which different perceptual reference frames become available.

- Your body is not the limit of perception.
- Your skin is not the boundary of awareness.

As your attention shifts, your system reorients.

What changes is not reality itself, but the reference frame through which information is accessed. As Ingo once observed, "Humans argue about reality. Reality continues anyway."

This chapter begins to map those frames.

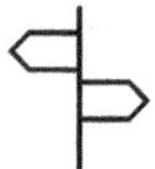

## Perceptual Reference Frames

Ingo described how ideas, understandings, and entire versions of reality function as frames of reference: internal orientations that determine what can be perceived, how it is organized, and what is recognized as meaningful.

Here, we are exploring reference frames prior to belief or concept.

These are not interpretations, but perceptual orientations that shape what information becomes available and how attention organizes around it.

Multiple reference frames can operate simultaneously.

They are not places you go, but orientations you recognize.

Each one changes the context in which perception organizes itself.

Shifting between them does not require effort. It requires recognition.

As attention moves, different patterns of information become more noticeable.

The five foundational reference frames explored in this section are:

1. The Personal Reference Frame
2. The Relational Reference Frame
3. The Environmental Reference Frame
4. The Collective Reference Frame
5. The Symbolic / Contextual Reference Frame

You move through all of them every day. Most people do so unconsciously.

Each frame organizes perception differently.

Here, the task is simply to notice which frame is organizing perception at a given moment.

Pause. Check resonance.

## 1. The Personal Reference Frame

*Your immediate perceptual orientation.*

This frame organizes information relative to your own body and internal state. It is structured around sensation: your posture, breath, emotional tone, and boundary integrity. It typically extends a few feet beyond the body and becomes more coherent as attention stabilizes.

You may recognize this frame when:

> you shift your posture after sensing tension in your shoulders
> your breath deepens before you consciously decide to slow down
> you notice your mood change before you understand why
> a room suddenly feels "too much," and you instinctively step back or ground yourself
> you pause and ask yourself, "What am I actually feeling right now?"

Within this frame, what you perceive is embodied, immediate, and largely literal. Information is processed in relation to your own regulation rather than in relation to others, environments, or symbolic meaning.

You have already explored this frame through:

> boundary sensing
> expansion and contraction
> warmth and pressure awareness
> emotional tone mapping
> perceptual coherence alignment

The Personal Reference Frame serves as your primary anchor. It determines whether information extends from stability or from fragmentation.

When this frame is coherent:

> signals are proportionate
> emotion is felt without distortion
> attention remains steady

When it weakens:

> external input overwhelms more easily
> other frames override grounding
> meaning forms without sufficient internal orientation

Example:

You receive a message that unsettles you.

Before responding, you pause and notice what is happening internally. Your breathing has shortened slightly, and there is a tightness in your stomach.

Rather than immediately interpreting the message or deciding what it means, your attention stays with these sensations. As you notice them, your breathing lengthens and your posture settles.

The situation itself has not changed. But your perception of it has reorganized.

In that moment, you are perceiving through the Personal Reference Frame. Your attention remains anchored in your own state before extending outward toward interpretation or response.

*Pause. Check resonance.*

## 2. The Relational Reference Frame
*Perception oriented toward between rather than within.*

When your attention shifts from "me" to "between," a shared perceptual context becomes available. Within this frame, signals begin organizing around interaction rather than internal regulation. Emotional frequency, shifts in attention, and subtle signaling often become perceptible before words appear.

You may recognize this frame when:

> a pause in conversation changes the atmosphere before anyone speaks
> eye contact shifts the tone of an interaction before language does
> someone's tension subtly alters your own breathing or posture
> a group's mood changes when a particular person enters the room
> you sense agreement, discomfort, or hesitation before it is spoken

Within this frame, what you perceive becomes interactive rather than internal. Signals are processed in relation to another person's system rather than solely in relation to your own.

You have already encountered aspects of this frame through:

> emotional interaction
> relational boundaries
> relational effects

The Relational Reference Frame allows your system to track dynamic exchange rather than isolated sensation. It reveals how meaning forms through interaction.

When this frame is coherent:

> interaction feels proportionate
> emotional tone is distinguishable from projection
> attention moves fluidly between people
> boundaries remain intact

When it destabilizes:

> another person's state overrides your own
> projection replaces discernment
> interaction feels draining, inflated, or confusing

Example:

You are speaking with someone about an ordinary topic.

The conversation is moving easily, and then something shifts. The other person pauses slightly before responding. Their posture changes, and the rhythm of the conversation slows.

Nothing explicit has been said, yet the atmosphere between you feels different.

Your attention moves from your own thoughts to the space between you. You begin registering timing, tone, and subtle changes in expression. The interaction itself becomes the information.

In that moment, you are perceiving through the Relational Reference Frame. Your system is tracking the exchange rather than focusing only on your internal state.

*Pause. Check resonance.*

## 3. The Environmental Reference Frame
*The perceptual atmosphere of places.*

This frame does not belong to the environment alone. It emerges when your system orients to place as a context rather than as a backdrop. Information begins organizing relative to spatial pattern, history of use, density of activity, and environmental tone.

You may recognize this frame when:

> entering a room and sensing tension before anyone speaks
> stepping into a quiet natural setting and feeling your breathing slow
> noticing that certain spaces consistently feel energizing, heavy, or calm
> sensing that the tone of a meeting shifts when the setting changes
> becoming aware that different environments affect your attention and mood differently

Within this frame, what you perceive organizes around environment rather than self or relationship. The place itself becomes part of the perceptual equation.

You have already encountered aspects of this frame through:

> room sensing
> threshold awareness
> corner mapping
> nature feedback

When your system orients to place as a reference frame, mood, memory, and residual tone may become noticeable. This does not mean the space "contains" emotion. It means your organismic intelligence is detecting patterned context across time.

When this frame is coherent:

> spatial tone is distinguishable from projection
> context clarifies rather than overwhelms
> environmental influence is sensed without absorption

When it destabilizes:

> atmosphere overrides internal regulation
> projection fills ambiguous space
> mood is attributed without discernment

Example:

You walk into a conference room where a meeting has just ended.

No one is speaking, yet the space feels tense and slightly unsettled. The chairs are still out of place, and the air feels charged.

Nothing explicit is happening, but your attention registers the room differently than it would an empty, neutral space. The environment itself becomes information.

In that moment, perception is organizing through the Environmental Reference Frame. Your system is responding to the spatial context rather than to your internal state or to a direct interaction with another person.

*Pause. Check resonance.*

## 4. The Collective Reference Frame
*Shared emotional and attentional organization.*

This reference frame organizes perception around group-level patterns rather than individual experience. Information begins to register relative to shared tone, social rhythm, and collective direction.

You may recognize this frame when:

⟩ a crowd's mood shifts suddenly, and everyone seems to register it at once
⟩ laughter spreads through a group faster than any individual reaction
⟩ a city or public gathering carries a distinct emotional tone
⟩ large-scale events alter the atmosphere beyond any one person
⟩ digital exchanges amplify urgency, outrage, or enthusiasm before the specifics are defined

Within this frame, what you perceive organizes around collective dynamics rather than personal sensation or individual interaction.

You have already encountered aspects of this frame through:

⟩ crowd awareness
⟩ group tone shifts
⟩ shared attention
⟩ amplification in collective settings

When your system orients this way, it begins registering patterns of shared attention and emotional rhythm across many people at once.

When this frame is coherent:

⟩ collective tone is distinguishable from personal emotion
⟩ influence is sensed without identification
⟩ awareness remains anchored while widened

When it destabilizes:

⟩ collective tone overrides internal regulation
⟩ identity fuses with group mood
⟩ discernment collapses into conformity or reactivity

Example:

You sit in a movie theater during a suspenseful scene. The room grows quiet as the tension builds. Without anyone speaking, the audience seems to inhale together. When the tension breaks, laughter or relief spreads almost instantly across the room.

No single person creates the shift, yet the shared atmosphere is unmistakable.

In that moment, perception is organizing through the Collective Reference Frame. Your attention registers the emotional rhythm of the group rather than focusing on any one individual.

*Pause. Check resonance.*

## 5. Symbolic / Contextual Reference Frame
*The most abstract perceptual reference frame.*

This is the most abstract reference frame. In this orientation, information appears in compressed, patterned, or symbolic form rather than through direct sensory input. It is not detached from the body, but it is less anchored to immediate physical context.

You may recognize this frame when:

> an image from a dream lingers without clear explanation
> a metaphor suddenly captures something you cannot yet articulate
> a pattern repeats across different situations and begins to feel meaningful
> a quiet sense of direction appears before events fully unfold
> understanding arrives as a simple recognition rather than as a chain of reasoning

Within this frame, perception organizes through accumulated context and pattern recognition across time rather than through immediate sensory proximity.

You have already encountered aspects of this frame through:

> symbolic impressions
> recurring imagery
> pattern recognition across situations
> moments of quiet clarity

When coherent, this frame is characterized by:

> stability rather than urgency
> neutrality rather than emotional charge
> compression rather than narrative
> receptive, non-forcing attention

When it destabilizes:

> imagination replaces pattern recognition
> narrative momentum overrides neutrality
> emotional charge amplifies symbolic content
> ambiguity fills with projection
> coherence gives way to premature interpretation

Example:

You wake from a dream with a clear image still present in your mind.

The meaning is not obvious, yet the image carries a distinct tone that lingers even after the details fade.

Later, a conversation or situation reminds you of the same image. The connection is not logical or literal, yet the pattern feels familiar.

In that moment, perception is organizing through the Symbolic / Contextual Reference Frame. Your system is registering meaning through pattern and association rather than through immediate sensory cues.

*Pause. Check resonance.*

## Why the Deep Background Matters

The perceptual reference frames described here operate continuously, whether or not they are consciously recognized. They form the deep background through which your system organizes input before your intellect intervenes.

When these reference frames are recognized, perception becomes:

> differentiated rather than confusing
> organized rather than random
> proportionate rather than overwhelming
> meaningful rather than chaotic

Without this background awareness, signals from different frames blend together. Personal emotion may be mistaken for collective tone. Symbolic information may be confused with imagination. Environmental atmosphere may be absorbed as identity.

The result is not a lack of perception, but misattribution.

Recognition changes this.

Instead of experiencing everything at once, you begin to notice:

> which reference frame perception is organizing from
> how information is presenting (literal, relational, environmental, collective, or symbolic)
> how much weight to give what you are perceiving
> when grounding is needed before expanding
> how to shift orientation deliberately rather than reactively

Clarity does not come from perceiving more. It comes from distinguishing what kind of perception is occurring and responding from the appropriate frame.

The deep background matters because it stabilizes perceptual orientation before interpretation begins. It allows your perceptual awareness system to broaden without fragmenting and meaning to emerge without distortion.

This chapter introduces a working map of this orientation.

It is not a model to adopt, but a way of noticing how your system is already organizing itself.

From that recognition, you can move between reference frames with steadiness rather than confusion.

*Pause. Check resonance.*

## EXPLORATION 12.1: Finding the Deep Quiet

The Entry Point into the Deep Background of Reference

### Objective

To allow your system to shift into a quieter orientation beneath immediate reaction.

### Setup

Sit or stand comfortably. Let your gaze soften. Allow your posture to be supported rather than maintained through effort.

### Steps

1. Lengthen your exhale.
   - → Breathe in for a slow count of 5, and out for a slow count of 5.
   - → Do this for several cycles without forcing depth.
2. Widen your attention.
   - → Let your attention open beyond a single point of focus.
   - → Put your attention on the whole of your body at once, then the space immediately around it. (This is Lantern Mode.)
3. Release any mental effort.
   - → Notice any subtle effort to think, monitor, or control.
   - → Let that effort recede without trying to stop thought.
4. Allow your body to quiet.
   - → Stay with your widened attention until what you perceive feels less busy and more even.
   - → Do not search for anything.
5. Rest here briefly.
   - → Remain in this quieter orientation for 20–60 seconds.

### What to Watch For

- › a gentle downward settling
- › a sense of internal spaciousness
- › reduced emotional charge
- › clarity without intensity
- › time feeling less urgent
- › insights arising quietly rather than insistently

## Reflection

- ↺ How did this quiet differ from relaxation or distraction?
- ↺ Did what you notice feel wider, slower, or more neutral?
- ↺ What changed when you stopped trying to notice anything in particular?

*What you're noticing.*

**EXPLORATION 12.2: Sensing the Collective Frame of Reference**
Perceiving Group Atmosphere Without Merging

## Objective

To recognize collective emotional tone as context rather than identity.

## Setup

Enter a public or shared space (a café, store, street, meeting, transit area, or online gathering). You are not attempting to read individuals. You are orienting to the shared background of interaction.

## Steps

1. Widen your attention.
   - → Let your attention include the whole space rather than any single person. (This is Lantern Mode.)
   - → Notice sound, movement, pacing, density.
2. Orient to context.
   - → Ask internally: *What is the overall tone here?*
   - → Notice pace (slow, hurried), texture (tense, loose), cohesion (scattered, focused).
   - → Do not search for causes or narratives.
3. Name lightly.
   - → Choose one or two simple descriptors (e.g., hurried, heavy, relaxed, brittle, buoyant).
   - → Keep your language provisional.
   - → Avoid personalizing or diagnosing.
4. Reorient.
   - → Step away physically or shift your attention back to your personal reference frame.
5. Recheck baseline.
   - → Shift your attention back to your internal reference points.
   - → Notice your own emotional tone separate from the group.
   - → Identify what feels distinctly yours again.

**What to Watch For**

> shifts in your emotional tone
> bodily responses (chest, stomach, breath)
> expansion or contraction of your attention
> changes in your energy or posture

**Reflection**

↺ Did the collective tone feel distinct from your personal state?
↺ How did your body signal the difference?
↺ What changed when you returned to your personal reference frame?

*What you're noticing.*

**EXPLORATION 12.3: Contextual Afterimage**
Symbolic Impressions Without Interpretation

## Objective

To recognize the texture of symbolic information when what your perceive is organized symbolically rather than literally.

## Setup

Begin from the Deep Quiet established in Exploration 12.1.

## Steps

1. Hold unfocused attention.
   - → Remain receptive without directing your attention toward any specific content.
   - → Notice what arises.
2. Allow impressions to appear naturally, such as:
   - → images or fragments
   - → shapes or spatial impressions
   - → words or phrases
   - → sensations or movement
   - → shifts in tone
3. Do not analyze.
4. Let impressions come and go without assigning meaning.
   - → Stay briefly.
   - → Remain receptive for 30–60 seconds, then return to ordinary awareness.

## What to Watch For

Impressions that are:

> light but vivid
> quiet but meaningful
> symbolic rather than literal
> emotionally neutral
> unfinished

**Reflection**

- ↺ Did the impression feel noticed rather than generated?
- ↺ Did the impression carry consistency without explanation?
- ↺ What happened when you did not try to understand it?

*What you're noticing.*

**INTEGRATION PRACTICE 12**
**Reference Frame Awareness**

Throughout the day, pause occasionally and ask: *Which reference frame is my system organizing from right now?*

> personal
> relational
> environmental
> collective
> symbolic / dimensional

You are not trying to change anything. Simply notice orientation. Differentiation brings clarity.

*Observations.*

**Closing Thought**

The world you inhabit is layered and participatory.

Your organismic intelligence evolved to navigate it.

Recognition of these reference frames is the beginning.

The next step is tracing the pathways between them: how information shifts from one frame to another while grounding and perceptual coherence are maintained.

# 13 | The Three Pathways of Perception
## How Information Arrives

### Opening Invitation

Organismic intelligence is not a single process.

It is organized through different pathways, depending on how information is registered, integrated, and translated into your awareness.

Every impression you receive (sensory, emotional, directional, or symbolic) enters your awareness through one primary route:

1. Literal perception
2. Inferential knowing, often described as a felt sense
3. Symbolic / dimensional perception

These are not levels of depth or importance.

They are distinct pathways of processing. Each one with its own texture, timing, and function.

Much of perceptual confusion arises not from sensing incorrectly, but from misidentifying the pathway through which the information arrived.

This chapter is about noticing how to tell the difference.

In a certain sense, it is probable that almost everyone can think of information as seeds. But few ever consider the condition or state of what the seeds must fall into.

— Ingo Swann, *The Superpower Faculties vs Maps of the Miind*

*What you're noticing.*

**Framing the Three Pathways**

## How the Three Pathways Operate

Information does not always arrive in a step-by-step sequence.

Often it registers all at once, as a whole pattern, before words, reasoning, or explanation form. This is one way non-linear perception can appear.

Non-linear does not mean vague, irrational, or unstructured. It means that information is not organized as a simple chain of causes but may arise as a complete configuration.

A non-linear impression may:

> contain relevance without explanation
> convey direction without narrative
> hold meaning without timeline
> register coherence before detail

Non-linear perception is not opposed to reason. It simply precedes it. Understanding may unfold later, through reflection or integration.

When perceptual pathways are differentiated, confusion dissolves. You stop blending:

> sensation with symbol
> awareness with fear
> perception with memory
> meaning with distortion
> symbolic material with imagination
> physical cues with emotional residue

When you know which pathway a perception belongs to, interpretation stops being guesswork. Response becomes appropriate rather than reactive.

What follows is not a hierarchy of perception, but a map of routes, a way of recognizing whether information arrived through the body, as inferential knowing, or as symbolic form, so it can be met at the right level.

## 1. Literal Perception

*Sensory-adjacent, present-moment, low distortion.*

Literal perception is the pathway through which information is experienced closest to direct physical and emotional immediacy.

It operates through sensory channels and near-sensory signals, allowing your organismic intelligence to register what is happening in the environment before interpretation or narrative forms.

Because this pathway is closely tied to immediate sensation, it tends to carry the least distortion.

Information appears in a relatively direct form and is processed in relation to the present moment rather than through memory, inference, or symbolic patterning.

Literal perception includes signals that arise through the senses as well as signals that register just beyond them: subtle shifts in proximity, tone, or spatial pressure that your system detects before your intellect organizes them.

This pathway may include:

> physical cues and movement
> body language and posture
> subtle sounds or changes in vocal tone
> shifts in environmental pressure or spatial proximity
> temperature changes or alterations in atmosphere
> someone entering your personal space
> direct sensory-like impressions
> certain forms of distant or indirect sensory awareness

In everyday life, literal perception appears whenever you notice something happening before you have time to interpret it, such as:

> sensing that someone has entered a room behind you;
> noticing tension in another person's posture before they speak; or
> detecting a change in the atmosphere of a space without immediately knowing why.


### How It Feels

> clear / neutral
> grounded / steady
> tangible

## Common Mistakes

> over-interpreting
> skipping literal cues
> turning sensation into symbolism

*Pause. Check resonance.*

## 2. Inferential Knowing
*Directional, pre-verbal, pattern-based.*

Inferential knowing is not symbolic. It is your system assembling fragments into perceptual coherence faster than your intellect can organize them. It does not present images or narratives. Instead, it appears as orientation: a sense of direction, relevance, or tendency before detail becomes clear.

This pathway operates through rapid pattern recognition. Your organismic intelligence detects subtle relationships among signals (timing, tone, movement, context) and begins organizing them into a preliminary understanding before conscious reasoning catches up.

Because this process happens quickly and often without language, it can feel like a quiet pull of attention rather than a clear thought.

This pathway may include:

> low-level pulls or nudges of attention
> "something's here" sensations without clear content
> a sense of direction without detail
> early pattern recognition across events or interactions
> awareness of likelihood or tendency before explanation
> knowing before details assemble

Inferential knowing often appears in ordinary situations: sensing that a conversation is shifting before anyone says why, recognizing that a situation is developing in a particular direction, or noticing that certain pieces of information fit together before you can explain how.

Most people rely on this pathway constantly.

They simply do not recognize it as perception because their intellects tends to claim the result after the pattern has already formed.

Inferential knowing is not guesswork. It is early-stage organization: meaning beginning to take shape before language or imagery completes the picture.

### How It Feels

> soft / subtle / emotionally light
> directional
> quietly certain

## Common Mistakes

> mistaking it for anxiety
> ignoring it because it lacks detail
> translating direction into imagery or story prematurely

*Pause. Check resonance.*

### 3. Symbolic Perception
*Symbolic, compressed, meaning-rich, non-literal.*

Symbolic perception is the pathway through which information is carried in form rather than in literal detail.

Instead of presenting facts or direct sensory cues, this pathway organizes meaning through pattern, imagery, relationship, and metaphor.

In symbolic perception, information is compressed. A single image, scene, or impression may represent multiple elements of a situation at once.

The meaning does not appear as a sequence of statements but as a pattern that becomes clearer as attention remains steady.

Because symbolic information is condensed in this way, it often arrives before explanation and may feel incomplete until it is recognized within a broader context.

This pathway may include:

> images that arise without deliberate thought
> symbolic impressions
> metaphorical scenes
> archetypal tone
> dreamlike fragments
> emotionally neutral but meaningful impressions
> non-linear organization of information

Symbolic perception often appears in dreams, spontaneous imagery, recurring metaphors, or moments when a simple image seems to carry more meaning than can be expressed directly.

Because this pathway organizes information through compression and association, it is powerful but also easily distorted.

Without grounding in literal and inferential perception, imagination, projection, and emotional charge can quickly replace signal.

For this reason, symbolic perception is best recognized after the other pathways are stable, not before.

When it appears within a regulated system, symbolic information can reveal patterns and relationships that are difficult to express through linear reasoning alone.

## How It Feels

> light but vivid  / quietly meaningful
> non-linear
> emotionally neutral or gently toned
> larger than personal memory

## Common Mistakes

> taking symbols literally
> rushing interpretation
> emotionalizing symbols
> dismissing symbols as imagination

*Pause. Check resonance.*

## Why Three Pathways Matter

When perceptual pathways aren't distinguished, people often:

⟩ take symbols literally
⟩ mistake inferential knowing for emotion
⟩ turn physical sensations into "messages"
⟩ inflate meaning through fear or memory
⟩ dismiss subtle cues as imagination

Confusion doesn't come from the information itself.

It comes from mixing pathways.

Four simple questions restore clarity:

1. Where did this arrive: through the body, as direction, or as symbolic form?
2. Is this registering the present moment, or a broader pattern unfolding over time?
3. Does this call for action, interpretation, or simple noticing?
4. Should this be held literally or lightly, as meaning?

## How to Separate the Pathways in Real Time

One guiding rule keeps perception clean:

**Literal → Inferential → Symbolic**

1. Check for literal sensory or bodily information first.
2. Then notice inferential or pattern-based knowing.
3. Only then explore symbolic meaning, if it arises naturally.

This sequence reduces distortion.

Perceptual clarity comes less from receiving better information and more from recognizing how information arrived.

When pathways are differentiated, the process becomes simpler, not more complex.

## EXPLORATION 13.1: Pathway Identification Practice

Information's Arrival

### Objective

To recognize which perceptual pathway an impression arrives through by distinguishing its texture, orientation, and impact rather than interpreting its meaning.

### Setup

Sit comfortably. Allow your breath to settle into a natural rhythm.

### Steps

1.  Orient to the present moment.
    → Bring your attention to your body and the immediate space around you.
2.  Invite perception.
    → Ask: *What am I detecting right now?* Do not search for content.
    → Let something become noticeable on its own.
3.  Notice how the impression arrives.
4.  Without naming meaning, observe its characteristics:
    → Literal → close, bodily, sensory-adjacent, or environmental.
    → Inferential → directional, leaning, suggestive, anticipatory.
    → Symbolic → wide, compressed, meaning-rich, non-literal.
5.  Let recognition emerge.
    → Do not decide quickly.
    → Allow the impression to reveal its pathway through its felt qualities.
6.  Name the pathway lightly.
    → Once it feels stabilized, label the route of arrival without further interpretations.

### What to Watch For

Use these descriptions as orientation points, not criteria to meet:

⟩   Literal impressions often arise near immediate sensation or environment (such as bodily awareness or nearby physical presence) though this may vary.

⟩　Inferential impressions are often noticed as directional or orienting, appearing as a sense of leaning, pausing, or a felt indication of importance, rather than as detailed content.

⟩　Symbolic impressions often appear with a sense of breadth or compression, where relevance is present before explanation and imagery may arise without a clear source.

In many cases, your body identifies the pathway of an impression before the intellect attempts to name or interpret it.

## Reflection

↺　Which pathway was easiest for you to recognize?

↺　Which felt more unfamiliar?

↺　What physical, spatial, or qualitative cue helped you identify how the information arrived?

↺　What became apparent about the impression's pathway before meaning or interpretation began to form?

59

## EXPLORATION 13.2: Pathway Shifting
How Perception Reorganizes

### Objective

To notice the qualitative differences between perceptual pathways and observe how your attention naturally reorganizes between them.

### Setup

Sit comfortably. Allow your breath to steady without regulating it.

### Steps

1. Orient to the literal pathway.
   - → Bring your attention to your body and immediate surroundings.
   - → Notice direct sensory or bodily information without interpreting it.
2. Allow inferential knowing to register.
   - → Widen your attention to include the overall context of the space without focusing on details.
   - → Notice any sense of direction, tendency, or orientation that registers before thought.
3. Allow symbolic perception, if it arises.
   - → Let your attention soften further.
   - → If imagery, symbolic form, or meaning-rich impressions appear, notice them without engaging or interpreting.
4. Move gently between orientations.
   - → Shift your attention back and forth between these pathways without forcing transitions.
   - → Let each orientation organize itself briefly before moving on.
5. Return to grounding.
   - → End by reorienting to the literal pathway: your body and immediate environment.

### What to Watch For

- ⟩ changes in how your attention organizes itself
- ⟩ differences in immediacy, directionality, or meaning
- ⟩ shifts in pace, clarity, or orientation
- ⟩ one pathway feeling more familiar or easier to return to

**Reflection**

- ↺ Were you able to note a shift in how what you noticed organized itself?
- ↺ What indicated that your attention had reorganized rather than moved?
- ↺ Did one pathway feel more habitual or easier to stabilize than the others?

*What you're noticing.*

# EXPLORATION 13.3: Deconstructing a Perception
Separating an Impression by Pathway

## Objective

To differentiate the perceptual pathways involved in a single impression, so meaning can be clarified without distortion.

## Setup

Sit in a stable posture. Allow your breath to find its own rhythm.

## Steps

1. Select an impression.
    - → Choose a recent experience that carried some charge or significance (a feeling, reaction, image, or sense of knowing).
2. Revisit it gently.
    - → Bring the impression to mind without re-engaging emotionally or trying to explain it.
3. Differentiate the pathways. Ask, one at a time:
    - → Literal: What physical, bodily, or environmental cues were present?
    - → Inferential: What sense of direction, tendency, or likelihood emerged before explanation?
    - → Symbolic (if present): What images, metaphors, or meaning-rich impressions appeared?
4. Name briefly.
    - → Describe what you notice from each pathway in a few simple words.
    - → Do not interpret or connect them yet.
5. Pause.
    - → Notice what changes when the impression is held in differentiated form.

## What to Watch For

- ⟩ changes in intensity or urgency
- ⟩ confusion easing as components are distinguished
- ⟩ one pathway feeling steadier than the others
- ⟩ meaning becoming more differentiated, more integrated, or less pressured

**Reflection**

- ↺ What shifted once the pathways were differentiated?
- ↺ Did any part of the impression lose urgency or emotional charge?
- ↺ Which pathway felt most reliable or grounding in this situation?

*What you're noticing.*

**INTEGRATION PRACTICE 13**
**Pathway Tracking**

For the next week, when any perceptual moment stands out, pause and ask: *Which pathway did this arrive through?*

1. Literal
2. Inferential
3. Symbolic

Do not analyze content. Simply notice the route of arrival. You are not trying to make information more complex. You are sorting it, so it can become simpler, clearer, and easier to respond to appropriately.

Clarity comes from identifying how information arrived, not from deciding what it means.

*Observations.*

**Closing Thought**

You are not limited to a single way of perceiving.

You gather information through multiple perceptual pathways, each serving a distinct function:

> Literal perception provides clarity.
> Inferential knowing provides direction.
> Symbolic perception provides meaning.

When these pathways are recognized and kept distinct, information becomes steadier, more accurate, and easier to trust.

This differentiation (recognizing how information presents itself before deciding what to do with it) was central to the work Ingo devoted his life to clarifying.

He was not describing a belief system or advancing a theory.

He was pointing toward a form of perceptual literacy: the ability to notice how signals arrive, how they organize in awareness, and how easily they can be confused, amplified, or misinterpreted if their pathway is not recognized first.

In the next chapter, we turn to symbolic perception: how it operates, how meaning organizes through it across time, and how to engage it without distortion or inflation.

# 14 | Symbolic Cognition
## Translating Meaning

**Opening Invitation**

At the surface of awareness, information often arrives in familiar ways:

> sensations you can feel
> emotions you can name
> signals you can link to what is present
> impressions tied to your immediate environment

But not all information can be carried through literal or inferential pathways.

When your system encounters information that is non-linear or not easily assembled sequentially, it often arrives in symbolic form.

Instead of words, facts, or direct sensory cues, it may appear as:

> scenes
> symbols
> metaphors
> images
> emotional textures
> archetypal patterns
> fragments of meaning

This is symbolic cognition.

Symbolic cognition is not random, and it is not guessing.

It is your organismic intelligence organizing information symbolically when sequential processing would be insufficient.

To work with symbolic perception without distortion, it helps to understand how and why this rendering takes shape.

**Note: Symbol Does Not Mean Imaginary**

In this book, symbol does not mean imaginary, mystical, or metaphorical in the usual sense:

> metaphors chosen by the intellect
> mystical imagery to be interpreted literally
> universal meanings imposed from outside

Instead, symbols emerge when your perceptual awareness system organizes information as pattern rather than sequence.

They are your system's way of carrying complexity without overload.

A symbol may appear as:

> an image
> a spatial arrangement
> a movement or gesture
> a color, shape, or direction
> a recurring pattern that carries meaning before words form

The meaning is not fixed.

It is relational and contextual, shaped by your own mind-map, history, body, and environment.

What matters is not what a symbol represents, but how it is being rendered.

# THE THREE MODES OF SYMBOLIC RENDERING

Symbolic impressions arise through
distinct internal mechanisms.

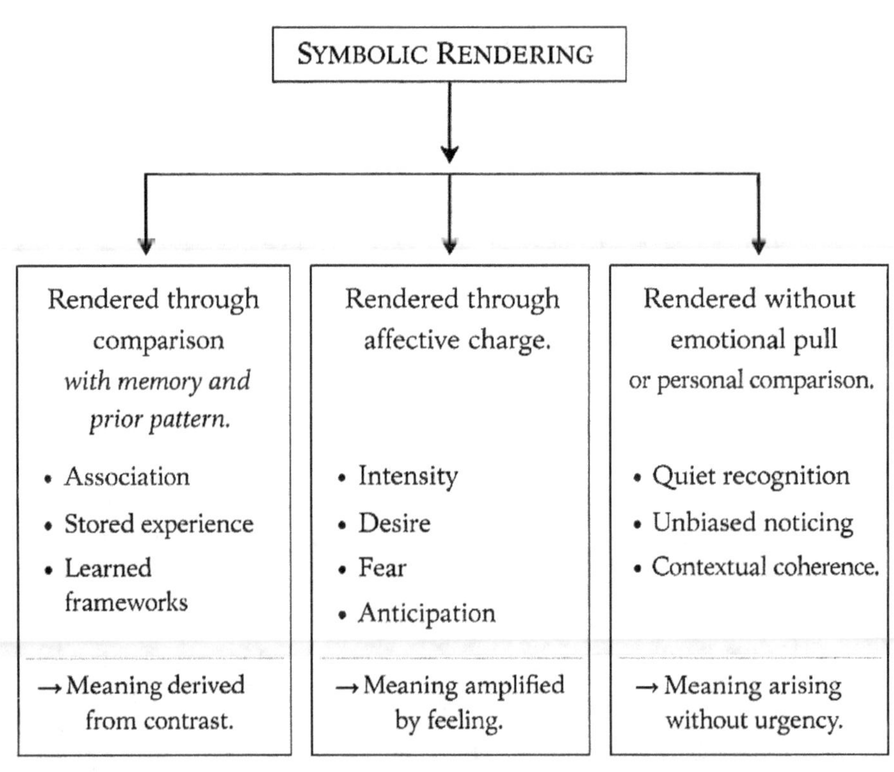

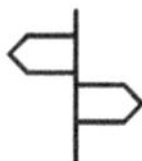

## The Three Modes of Symbolic Rendering

Symbolic impressions arise through different internal mechanisms.

1. **Comparator-Based Symbolic Rendering**
   Often traceable to prior experience or stored associations.

2. **Emotionally Generated Symbolic Rendering**
   Influenced by unresolved feeling, expectation, or desire.

3. **Neutral Symbolic Rendering**
   Arises without emotional pull or personal comparison.

Each mode generates meaning.

But they do not generate meaning in the same way.

> Confusing emotionally generated symbols for neutral ones leads to inflation.
> Confusing comparator-based symbols for insight leads to projection.
> Discernment prevents distortion.

The question is not whether a symbol is meaningful.

The question is how it was rendered.

## 1. Comparator-Based Symbolic Rendering: Translation Through Familiarity

This is the mechanism Ingo diagrammed extensively.

When unfamiliar, abstract, or non-sequential information reaches awareness, your system searches for correspondence.

It implicitly asks:

*What is this most like?*

To stabilize the signal, it:

> scans memory
> generates metaphor
> borrows familiar imagery
> assembles narrative-like structure

This process occurs because awareness cannot easily hold raw, non-linear information. In order for the signal to remain accessible, your system translates it into forms that your perceptual and cognitive structures already recognize.

This is not imagination in the ordinary sense. It is a stabilization process. The comparator translates unfamiliar pattern into familiar form so your system can hold the signal without fragmentation.

Because the originating information may not be visual or sequential, the translation often appears as imagery or symbolic form drawn from personal memory and experience.

This is why symbolic impressions may appear as:

> tunnels
> waves
> light
> shapes
> people or places...

...even when the originating information was not visual.

Comparator-based symbols tend to feel:

> personal
> memory-adjacent
> emotionally colored
> familiar
> story-like

This process differs from dreaming in several important ways.

Dreams arise primarily from internally generated material: memory consolidation, emotional processing, and narrative construction during sleep.

Comparator-based rendering occurs within waking awareness and functions as a translation mechanism, converting incoming pattern into recognizable form while perception remains regulated and grounded.

The key distinction is this: the symbol is a metaphor generated for comprehension, not a literal depiction of the information itself. The imagery belongs to your memory system; the pattern it carries does not.

## 2. Emotionally Generated Symbolic Rendering: Symbols Reflecting Internal State

Not all symbolic imagery reflects incoming information. Sometimes it reflects your system's internal response to that information.

In these cases, the symbol is not translating pattern. It is expressing regulation.

When emotional activation rises, your body often organizes sensation before your intellect identifies what is happening.

Pressure, contraction, warmth, or agitation may appear first as bodily shifts.

Symbolic imagery can emerge as a way for the system to express and organize those shifts.

Rather than translating an external signal into familiar form, the symbol externalizes internal state. It gives shape to feeling so awareness can register the condition of the system.

For example:

> fear may appear as darkness, storms, or enclosure
> hope may appear as light, openness, or forward movement
> pressure may appear as compression or crowding

These are sensory metaphors for internal state. They translate emotional tone into imagery that awareness can recognize.

Emotionally generated symbols tend to feel:

> vivid
> immersive
> emotionally charged
> atmospheric

Because they arise from internal activation, they often feel immediate and compelling. The imagery may describe the state of the system rather than the structure of the situation.

In contrast to comparator-based symbolic rendering, which translates unfamiliar pattern into recognizable imagery, emotionally generated symbols reflect the body's regulatory response to what is being encountered.

Recognizing this difference is essential. Without it, internal emotional state can easily be mistaken for external signal, and symbolic clarity collapses into projection.

*Pause. Check resonance.*

## 3. Neutral Symbolic Rendering: Low-Emotion, Meaning-Rich Impressions

Some symbolic impressions arise with little emotional charge and minimal personal reference.

These impressions do not appear as translations of familiar imagery, nor as expressions of emotional state.

Instead, they reflect a form of symbolic compression in which information organizes itself into pattern before narrative or interpretation develops.

Because little emotional activation is present, your system does not need to stabilize the signal through metaphor or regulation.

The result is imagery that often feels simpler and structurally distinct from imagination.

These impressions tend to:

> arrive whole rather than assembled
> feel clear without drama
> lack obvious memory association
> carry meaning without narrative
> feel structurally distinct from imagination

They may appear as:

> abstract or geometric forms
> archetypal patterns
> unfamiliar landscapes
> colors or qualities difficult to name
> symbols that carry relevance without story

These are not psychological metaphors in the usual sense:

> They are not expressions of emotion.
> They are not assembled from familiar imagery.

Instead, they reflect symbolic compression: information organized as pattern when it cannot be conveyed literally or inferentially.

Because these impressions carry little emotional charge, they often feel more concentrated, cohesive, and stable than emotionally generated imagery.

Their clarity tends to come from low interference rather than dramatic intensity.

## Symbolic Cognition in Waking Awareness

Symbolic cognition is adaptive.

When information cannot easily move through literal sensing or inferential pattern recognition, your system compresses and structures it symbolically so your awareness can hold the signal without overload.

Dreaming uses a related mechanism.

During dreaming the brain generates vivid imagery while the systems that maintain waking orientation to the environment and social context are largely offline. Experience reorganizes through symbolic form while awareness is immersed within it.

Symbolic cognition uses the same capacity for compression, but it operates during waking perception.

Attention remains stable, orientation to the environment is intact, and symbolic material appears within awareness rather than replacing it. In other words, dreaming places you inside the symbolic field. Symbolic cognition allows you to perceive symbolic structure while remaining awake and oriented.

## How to Recognize Symbolic Information

An impression is likely symbolic when:

1. It arrives whole rather than building gradually.
2. Meaning outweighs emotional charge.
3. It carries a quality of "otherness."
4. It fades under forceful analysis.
5. You remember the essence more than the details.
6. It does not follow linear time or logic.

Symbolic impressions are associative, not sequential; they organize meaning by pattern rather than by timeline.

## How to Work with Symbolic Perception Without Distortion

Change the framing from "interpretation" to engagement.

Before asking what it means, ask:

> What is the quality of this symbol?
> Does it feel personal, emotional, or neutral?
> Does it clarify with time, or intensify with attention?

Avoid asking:

> Is this a message?
> Is this predicting something?

Symbols point to patterns and qualities, not direct events.

*Pause. Check resonance.*

## Separating Symbol from Emotion

Before interpreting, ask: *Did this image come from my state, or in response to something beyond it?*

A usual working guideline:

> highly charged → often emotionally generated
> familiar or memory-linked → often comparator-based
> neutral yet meaningful → often cleaner symbolic rendering

This distinction alone dramatically improves clarity.


## When Symbols Are Taken Too Literally

When symbolic cognition is engaged too quickly, distortion often begins silently.

Common signs include:

> metaphor being unconsciously treated as fact
> pattern recognition mistaken for confirmation
> emotionally charged frameworks acquiring a sense of certainty
> personal meaning projected onto imagined agents, forces, or systems

These are not signs of organismic perception.

They are signs that symbolic material is being engaged before it has been grounded, differentiated by pathway, or allowed to organize over time.

Symbolic impressions are meaning-rich, but they are not self-interpreting.


## From Distortion to Misinterpretation

Without symbolic literacy, organismic perception often breaks down in predictable ways:

1. Over-literalizing → treating symbols as facts or predictions.
2. Dismissal → rejecting subtle information because it isn't concrete.
3. Distortion → forcing meaning too quickly.
4. Inflation → mistaking symbolic perception for special status or certainty.

Symbolic literacy keeps your organismic intelligence:

> Flexible rather than rigid.
> Curious rather than dogmatic.
> Grounded rather than abstract.

**Let Symbolic Impressions Breathe**

Do not force meaning. Let the symbol sit in your passive awareness. Instead, notice recurrence, resonance, patterning, and contextual fit.

Meaning stabilizes through repetition, coherence, and time.

Symbolic cognition unfolds.

Do not rush it.

**Stay Grounded**

Maintain connection with your breath, body, environment, emotional clarity, and literal perception.

Symbolic cognition is a tool, not an authority.

*Pause. Check resonance.*

## EXPLORATION 14.1: Symbol Texture Differentiation

The Rendering of Symbolic Meaning

### Objective

To distinguish how symbolic impressions are being rendered by noticing texture, tone, and bodily impact rather than interpreting content or assigning meaning.

### Setup

Sit comfortably. Allow your breath to proceed unmodified. Soften your gaze or close your eyes. Let your posture be supported rather than held.

### Steps

1. Before beginning, shift your attention inward and notice what feels slightly charged, unresolved, or present without emphasis. Symbols often organize around subtle salience rather than deliberate search.
2. Allow an impression to arise.
   - → Rather than generating imagery, bring to mind a recent moment that felt meaningful, ambiguous, or slightly "charged."
   - → Alternatively, notice whether an image, phrase, memory fragment, or symbolic form is already hovering at the edge of your awareness.
   - → Do not attempt to improve or clarify it.
   - → If nothing arises, remain with the sense of "waiting" itself; sometimes the texture of anticipation is the first signal.
3. Attend to its texture rather than its content.
   - → Notice how the impression feels in your body.
   - → Is it dense or light? Expansive or narrow?
   - → Does your attention move toward it, away from it, or around it?
   - → Stay with sensation rather than story.
4. Ask which of the following best describes how the impression is organizing:
   - → Emotionally rendered: Does it carry noticeable emotional charge, immersion, or mood shift?
   - → Comparator-based rendering: Does it feel familiar, memory-adjacent, or story-like, using recognizable imagery?
   - → Neutral symbolic rendering: Does it feel relatively neutral, clear, and quietly meaningful, without strong emotion or personal reference?

5. Notice without deciding.
   - → You are not classifying for accuracy.
   - → You are observing how your system translates experience into symbolic form.
   - → Stay with the texture a few moments longer than feels necessary.
6. Return to grounding.
   - → Reorient to your body and immediate surroundings.

## What to Watch For

- ⟩ how emotional charge (or lack of it) influences the impression
- ⟩ whether the symbol feels assembled from familiarity or arrives whole
- ⟩ effects on your breath, posture, or internal pacing
- ⟩ how recognition changes when interpretation is set aside

## Reflection

- ↺ What differences did you notice in how symbolic impressions were rendered?
- ↺ Which mode of rendering was easiest to recognize for you?
- ↺ What shifted when you stopped trying to interpret meaning and simply noticed texture?

What you're noticing.

What you're noticing.

**EXPLORATION 14.2: Symbol Deconstruction**
Structure Without Story

Think of a moment when an image stayed with you longer than its literal content warranted.

## Objective

To experience symbolic impressions as structured information rather than narrative, prediction, or explanation.

## Setup

Adopt a position that feels stable. Let your breathing regulate naturally. Soften your visual focus or close your eyes. Release excessive effort from your posture.

## Steps

1. Select a symbolic impression.
    → Choose an image, symbol, or meaning-rich impression from a dream, meditation, memory, conversation, or unexpected moment during the day.
2. Differentiate its components. Without interpreting meaning, notice the following aspects:
    → Qualitative Texture
        ÷ warm / cool
        ÷ sharp / soft
        ÷ heavy / light
        ÷ still / moving
        ÷ inward / outward
    → Tone
        ÷ neutral
        ÷ emotionally charged
        ÷ quietly meaningful
        ÷ unsettling
        ÷ comforting
    → Mode of Symbolic Rendering
        ÷ emotionally rendered
        ÷ comparator-based
        ÷ neutral symbolic

→ Possible Function (optional)
  ÷ orienting
  ÷ contextual
  ÷ clarifying
  ÷ cautioning
  ÷ confirming
  ÷ unknown

3. Name briefly.
   → Describe only what is present.
   → Avoid building story or explanation.
4. Pause.
   → Notice what shifts when structure is acknowledged and narrative is set aside.

## What to Watch For

⟩ intensity often softening as structure replaces story
⟩ clarity sometimes increasing even as certainty decreases
⟩ urgency changing when the rendering mode is recognized
⟩ meaning becoming quieter, steadier, or less insistent

## Reflection

↻ What changed when you focused on structure rather than narrative?
↻ Did recognizing the rendering mode affect how much authority the symbol carried?
↻ What remained when interpretation was set aside?

*What you're noticing.*

*What you're noticing.*

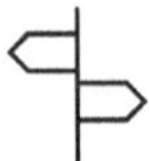

## Cognitive Overlay as a Category of Noise

In Book Two, perceptual information intake was described as a signal-to-noise problem, how interference competes with a signal before recognition. Here, we examine how meaning itself can become part of that interference.

Noise includes rumination, prediction, internal commentary, and repetitive cognitive looping: mental activity that crowds out signals before they can be spotted.

Cognitive overlay is a more specific form of noise.

Where looping introduces competing volume, overlay introduces competing meaning.

Cognitive overlay occurs when the intellect encounters fragmentary or incomplete data and rapidly fills in the blanks.

> A faint impression becomes a named object.
> A symbolic fragment becomes a story.
> An emotional tone becomes a conclusion.

Because symbolic information often appears incomplete or ambiguous at first, the intellect may attempt to resolve it prematurely by supplying familiar imagery, memories, or logical conclusions

Within the Controlled Remote Viewing (CRV) protocols developed by Ingo, this tendency was referred to as Analytic Overlay (AOL): the conscious mind's attempt to resolve ambiguous perceptual signals by supplying imagery, memory, or logical deduction.

The phenomenon, however, is not limited to that context.

It is a general feature of human cognition under uncertainty.

Cognitive overlay is not a flaw. It is a stabilizing function. The intellect prefers coherence to ambiguity, and completion to openness.

Signals often arrives as fragments, textures, directions, or tones. Cognitive overlay arrives as explanation.

Cognitive overlay does not distort by being loud; it distorts by being convincing.

*Pause. Check resonance.*

## EXPLORATION 14.3: Neutral Symbolic Entry Point

Symbolic Perception Without Emotional Charge

### Objective

To experience symbolic perception as it first takes form, with minimal emotional or cognitive overlay. The emphasis is on receptivity rather than completion, allowing impressions to remain incomplete and lightly held. In this space, you experience how interpretation attaches itself, and how rendering becomes embellishment.

### Setup

Sit in a way that feels stable and supported. Allow your breath to regulate on its own.

### Steps

1. Shift into receptivity.
   - → Soften your attention.
   - → Do not search for symbols or imagery.
   - → Let your system be available rather than directed.

2. Reestablish perceptual coherence.
   - → Briefly orient to internal steadiness.
   - → Feel your posture, breath, and boundary as stable reference points.

3. Reduce effort.
   - → Let unnecessary mental activity recede.
   - → Allow your attention to widen without targeting any object.

4. Sustain open attention.
   - → Remain available to whatever becomes perceptible.
   - → Do not anticipate, evaluate, or improve what appears.

5. Notice emergence, if any.
   - → An image, form, texture, directional sense, or quiet meaning may arise.
   - → Nothing may arise.
   - → Both are valid observations.

6. Reground deliberately.
   - → Reorient to yourself to your immediate surroundings.
   - → Confirm baseline stability before ending the practice.

## What to Watch For

> impressions that register quietly rather than insistently
> meaning present without strong emotional charge
> impressions that feel complete rather than assembled
> a lack of urgency to interpret or explain
> the absence of imagery as a valid perceptual outcome

## Reflection

↻ How did this experience differ from emotionally charged or memory-linked imagery?
↻ Did anything register as meaningful without explanation?
↻ What quality, if any, remained after you stopped attending to the impression?

*What you're noticing.*

# INTEGRATION PRACTICE 14
## Symbol Journaling

For the next week (or a period of time of your choice), record symbolic impressions using four simple labels.

Keep entries brief. This is a practice of recognition, not interpretation.

1.  Mode of Rendering (emotional, comparator-based, neutral symbolic)
2.  Qualitative Texture (texture, movement, density, openness, atmosphere)
3.  Tone (neutral, emotionally charged, quietly meaningful, unsettled, calm)
4.  Possible Function (if any) (orienting, clarifying, stabilizing, cautioning, confirming, unknown)

Do not try to resolve meaning immediately. Let patterns reveal themselves over time through repetition, perceptual coherence, or fading.

This practice builds symbolic literacy by strengthening your ability to notice how meaning is rendered before deciding what, if anything, it means.

*Observations.*

## Closing Thought

Symbols are not puzzles you must solve to be "right." They are bridges, a way meaning is carried when information cannot arrive literally or sequentially.

Symbolic cognition often sits at the intersection of:

> sensory reality
> inferential knowing
> symbolic meaning
> emotional state

Its function is not to deliver answers, but to hold complexity in a form your organismic intelligence can integrate.

What matters is not forcing interpretation, but becoming more fluent in the language your perceptual awareness system already uses: through recognition, patience, and consistency.

When symbolic cognition is understood in this way, your organismic perception remains:

> grounded
> accurate
> meaningful
> safe
> well-formed

In the next chapter, we turn to distortion: how it forms, why it persists, and how to stay oriented when what you perceive deepens without losing stability.

# 15 | Distortion, Interference, & Noise
## The Loss of Clarity & How to Restore It

### Opening Invitation

By now, you've navigated through how to notice:

> your own perceptual orientation
> relational dynamics between yourself and others
> environmental tone
> emotional influence on sensing
> the movement of attention
> symbolic rendering of meaning

At some point, a natural question arises: "Why does my perception feel clear and accurate at times, and unreliable at others?"

This chapter addresses that question directly.

Distortion is not failure.

Distortion is predictable.

It follows recognizable patterns:

> emotional interference
> boundary weakening
> cognitive overlay
> personal bias
> symbolic inflation
> attentional residue
> stress-related noise
> fatigue
> desire-driven interpretation
> comparator overreach
> symbolic compression under load

You are not meant to eliminate distortion. You are meant to recognize it.

Once recognized, most distortion loses its influence immediately.

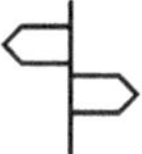

## Why Distortion Happens

Perceptual distortion does not result from the perceptual-awareness interchange process itself.

It arises when regulatory, emotional, cognitive, attentional, or interpretive framework processes interfere with how information is rendered and differentiated.

The signal itself may still be present, but interference alters how it stabilizes into meaning.

*Pause. Check resonance.*

Perception itself follows an orderly process.

Distortion arises when emotional, regulatory, cognitive, symbolic, or framework interference disrupts how information stabilizes into meaning.

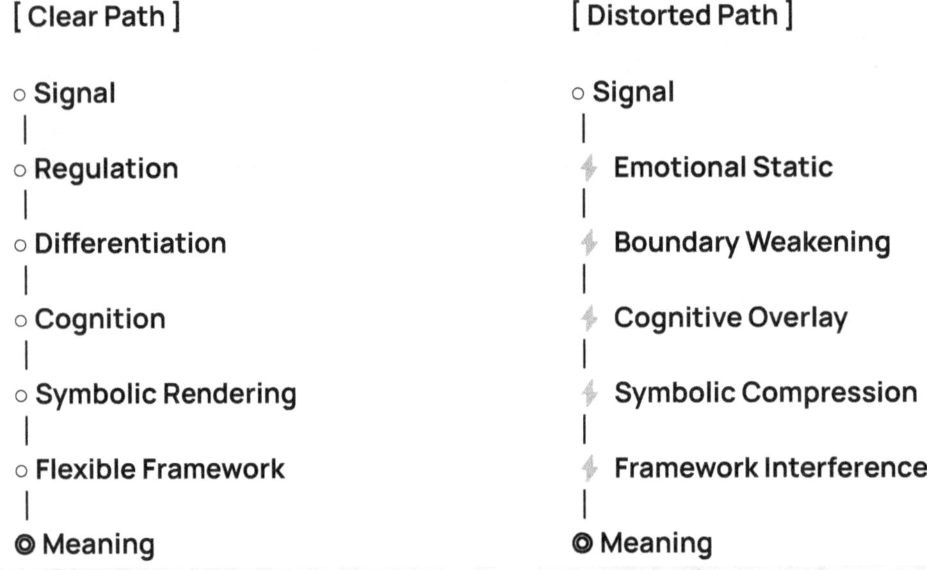



Following are eight common patterns.

Each has a distinct texture: a noticeable way it feels when it is happening.

Understanding these textures matters more than memorizing definitions.

*Pause. Check resonance.*

## 1. Emotional Static: When Emotional Load Overrides Perceptual Clarity

Emotional static occurs when emotional intensity rises faster than your system's capacity to regulate it.

*You may recognize this when…*

> a brief message immediately feels threatening or urgent
> someone's tone seems sharper than it likely was

Emotion itself is not the problem, undifferentiated emotion is.

When emotional load accumulates beyond what your system can currently stabilize, emotional tone begins shaping interpretation before the information has been fully differentiated.

Instead of allowing sensation and texture to organize gradually, your system resolves meaning through the emotional state already present.

It often appears as:

> fear narrowing what is perceivable
> desire inflating interpretation
> anger sharpening contrast
> anxiety accelerating conclusions
> sadness reducing resolution

Common signs include:

> rapid or compelled meaning-making
> bodily tightening or compression
> dramatic or charged symbolic imagery
> impressions skipping directly to conclusion
> a sense of urgency or inevitability

In this state, information may feel vivid or convincing, yet reliability drops.

Your system is reacting rather than registering.

Clarity returns when your emotional tone is regulated before interpretation resumes:

> returning first to emotional regulation rather than interpretation
> allowing the tone to settle before assigning meaning

Even brief regulation (slowing your breath, restoring posture, reestablishing boundary) often reduces static enough for your system to reorganize on its own.

Accuracy returns not through effort, but through stability.

*Pause. Check resonance.*

## 2. Cognitive Overlay: When Thought Moves Ahead of Perception

Cognitive overlay becomes distorting not because thought exists, but because it moves out of sequence.

Your perceptual awareness system organizes information in stages.

1. Sensation differentiates.
2. Tone stabilizes.
3. Form takes shape.

Analytic interpretation belongs later in this sequence.

*You may recognize this when…*

⟩ you find yourself explaining what something means before fully noticing what happened

When interpretation arrives before this organization has matured, meaning stabilizes prematurely. Instead of allowing sensation and tone to differentiate fully, your intellect begins assembling explanation.

Overlay in this context is less about volume and more about timing. The distortion lies in acceleration. Thought is not the problem. Sequence is.

It often appears as:

⟩ explanation forming before sensation has differentiated
⟩ narrative assembling before texture clarifies
⟩ certainty arriving before perceptual resolution
⟩ "I know what this means" before the signal has fully taken shape

When interpretation precedes sufficient perceptual organization, the resulting explanation may feel coherent while remaining incomplete. In this state your system stabilizes around a partial rendering of the signal.

Clarity returns when order is reestablished rather than when cognition is suppressed:

⟩ remain with the sensation before concluding
⟩ track the tone and texture before assigning meaning
⟩ allow differentiation before explanation
⟩ let form stabilize before narrative attaches

When your organismic intelligence completes its own sequence, meaning arrives with less urgency and greater precision.

The information feels less amplified, more proportionate, and less defended.

*Pause. Check resonance.*

99

*Pause. Check resonance.*

### 3. Comparator Inflation: When Familiar Imagery Over-Replaces the Signal

Comparator inflation occurs when your system encounters an unclear or compressed signal and immediately substitutes familiar imagery in order to stabilize it.

Your perceptual awareness system naturally uses comparison to interpret unfamiliar information. When a signal is ambiguous, your system searches memory for something similar so your intellect can hold it without losing coherence.

This process is normally helpful. It allows unfamiliar information to become understandable through metaphor or resemblance.

Inflation occurs when the comparison expands beyond its stabilizing role.

Instead of holding the signal lightly as "similar to something," your system replaces the signal with the familiar image itself. Ambiguity is resolved too quickly, and the comparison becomes the interpretation.

*You may recognize this when...*

⟩    someone reminds you of a person from your past and you begin interpreting them through that similarity

What begins as orientation becomes substitution. The original signal is not clarified; it is overridden.

It often appears as:

⟩    a fleeting signal expanding into a detailed scene
⟩    neutrality filling with personal memory
⟩    texture becoming character
⟩    symbol being treated as literal depiction

This process relates directly to Chapter 14, where symbolic cognition is examined in greater depth.

Clarity returns when the comparator is returned to its proper function: orientation rather than replacement:

⟩    explicitly noting: "This is like something, not literally that."
⟩    allowing the symbol to remain symbolic rather than explanatory
⟩    returning to the underlying tone before narrative forms

Symbols belong to symbolic cognition, not literal perception. When held in their proper domain, they remain useful without becoming inflated or misleading.

*Pause. Check resonance.*

## 4. Boundary Weakening: When Another's State Blends with Your Own

Boundary weakening occurs when perceptual containment softens beyond what your system can currently hold.

*You may recognize this when...*

> you leave a conversation carrying an emotional tone that wasn't originally yours

In this state, external emotional or attentional signals enter your awareness without sufficient differentiation.

Perceptual boundaries normally allow your system to register relational signals while maintaining orientation to your own internal state. They function as containment rather than separation.

When containment weakens, signals from another person or environment begin blending with your own internal baseline.

Instead of recognizing the signal as relational information, your system absorbs it as personal experience.

It often appears as:

> another's emotion felt as your own
> loss of internal neutrality
> interpretation becoming subtly colored or biased

This is loss of differentiation, not empathy.

Empathy refers to the capacity to participate in another's feelings or ideas while remaining aware that the experience is not your own. It allows resonance without surrendering orientation.

When boundaries weaken, that orientation disappears. What begins as resonance shifts into absorption, and another person's emotional state is experienced as if it were your own.

Clarity returns when perceptual containment is restored:

> reorienting your attention to your own body and internal baseline
> restoring your perceptual containment using the boundary practices from Chapter 11

Containment does not reduce sensitivity, it stabilizes it.

Clarity requires containment, not separation.

## 5. Attentional Residue: When Attention Remains Oriented After Interaction

Attentional residue occurs when your attention remains partially oriented toward a person, situation, or perceptual frame after the interaction itself has ended.

*You may recognize this when...*

> hours later your attention keeps returning to a conversation that already ended

The signal may have passed, but the attentional linkage has not fully released.

Attention naturally forms temporary orientation during interaction. This orientation allows your system to track relational, emotional, or environmental signals as they unfold.

When interaction concludes, that orientation normally relaxes and returns to baseline.

Residue occurs when this release does not fully complete.

Instead of resetting, part of your attention remains connected to the earlier interaction, allowing impressions from that interaction to continue influencing your present perception.

It often appears as:

> lingering bodily responses or activation
> symbolic material blending with present context
> impressions feeling "sticky" or hard to clear
> uncertainty about whether information belongs to now or earlier

This is not increased sensitivity. Instead, it is incomplete disengagement.

Clarity returns when attentional orientation is allowed to release and return to present reference by:

> consciously releasing attentional orientation
> returning your attention to present-moment sensory reference (body, breath, environment)

Attention releases more reliably through gentleness than force.

When orientation completes, your system resets naturally.

## 6. Stress, Fatigue, & Load: When Capacity Drops Below Resolution

Stress, fatigue, and cognitive load reduce your system's available processing capacity.

*You may recognize this when…*

⟩ something that would normally be clear feels unusually difficult to interpret

When capacity drops below what a signal requires for clear differentiation, perceptual resolution decreases. Information may still be present, but your system cannot organize it with sufficient clarity.

Instead of arriving as differentiated texture and form, signals begin to blur or flatten.

It often appears as:

⟩ perceptual resolution decreases
⟩ signals blur or flatten
⟩ symbolic material becomes noisy or indistinct

This is not distortion; it is reduced capacity.

Your perceptual-awareness interchange continues operating, but your system does not have sufficient resources to process information at full resolution.

Clarity returns through restoring capacity rather than increasing effort:

⟩ rest and recovery
⟩ grounding in bodily sensation
⟩ regulating and slowing your breath
⟩ adequate sleep
⟩ simplifying your attention rather than expanding it

Perceptual accuracy depends on available capacity.

Clarity cannot be forced through exhaustion.

## 7. Symbolic Compression: When Meaning Becomes Over-Simplified Under Load

Symbolic compression occurs when incoming information exceeds your system's current processing capacity.

*You may recognize this when...*

⟩ a single image or phrase seems to carry more meaning than you can immediately explain

When this happens, meaning does not disappear.

It condenses.

Instead of arriving as sequential detail, information is rendered symbolically so your system can hold it without overload.

It often appears as:

⟩ complex meaning → symbol
⟩ symbol → metaphor
⟩ metaphor → image

Nothing is wrong.

This is an adaptive rendering.

Your system is carrying more information than it can currently hold intact, so meaning arrives in condensed form rather than expanded explanation.

Distortion occurs only when compressed meaning is forced into premature interpretation.

Clarity returns when compression is allowed to unfold naturally:

⟩ strengthening grounding and regulation
⟩ developing symbolic literacy (holding symbol(s) without literalizing it/them)
⟩ allowing time for meaning to unfold

As capacity increases, compression resolves naturally.

Detail returns without force.

## 8. Framework Interference: When Belief Structures Pre-Shape Meaning

Framework interference occurs when the interpretive structures already present in your system resolve ambiguity before what is perceived can be fully differentiated.

Perceptual information arrives shaped by prior experience, emotional learning, cultural context, and belief. Together these influences form the framework through which meaning organizes.

*You may recognize this when...*

⟩ a situation seems to confirm something you already believed without much reflection

Frameworks are not inherently problematic. They allow data to stabilize quickly enough for ordinary functioning. Without them, every signal would require complete reconstruction.

Distortion occurs when a framework stabilizes meaning before your system has completed its own sequence. Instead of allowing sensation, tone, and form to differentiate, your system resolves the signal through what it already expects.

It often appears as:

⟩ unfamiliar signals dismissed quickly
⟩ ambiguous information resolved through assumption
⟩ interpretation feeling obvious or immediate
⟩ conclusions forming before perceptual texture clarifies

When this happens, the resulting meaning may feel coherent and convincing. Yet the clarity reflects the strength of the framework rather than the accuracy of what has been perceived.

Framework interference is rarely deliberate. It operates through familiarity. Belief structures reinforce what they already recognize and filter what does not easily fit their pattern.

Clarity returns when interpretation is allowed to stabilize more gradually:

⟩ remain with the sensation before explanation forms
⟩ notice assumptions without immediately correcting them
⟩ allow ambiguity to remain present long enough for differentiation

The task is not to eliminate belief. It is to recognize when belief has stabilized meaning too quickly. The deeper structures through which belief organizes perception will be explored in greater detail in Book Five.

*Pause. Check resonance.*

## How to Recognize Distortion in Real Time

Five reliable indicators:

1. Urgency: clarity does not rush
2. Emotional spike: intensity lowers resolution
3. Dramatic imagery: clarity is usually neutral
4. Bodily contraction: distortion tightens
5. Desire: wanting something to be true (or false) introduces bias

If one or more are present: pause.

Clarity returns under pause, not pressure.

## The Distortion Compass

When information feels unclear, ask:

1. Where is my attention oriented right now?
2. Is my body steady, or contracted?
3. What emotional tone is present?
4. Am I sensing, or already interpreting?
5. Is the symbolic material neutral or charged?
6. Does this feel immediate, or borrowed from context, memory, or expectation?

This prevents most distortion before it hardens into belief.

## Anchor

Distortion accelerates. It moves faster than differentiation can support.

Clarity stabilizes. It arrives after your perceptual awareness system has completed its own organization.

When meaning feels urgent, restore sequence.

When it feels proportionate, it is more likely accurate.

*Pause. Check resonance.*

## EXPLORATION 15.1: Distortion Diagnosis
When Your System Loses Clarity

### Objective

To recognize the early bodily and perceptual signatures of distortion so they can
be noticed sooner in real time.

### Setup

Adopt a quiet, supported posture. Allow your breath to find its natural cadence.

### Steps

1.  Recall a past instance of misperception.
    → Bring to mind a time when your interpretation later proved inaccurate or
      incomplete.
2.  Identify the dominant distortion pattern.
    → Without judgment, notice which type was most active (emotional static,
      cognitive overlay, comparator inflation, boundary weakening, attentional
      residue, fatigue, symbolic compression, or framework interference).
3.  Revisit the bodily experience.
    → Recall how your body felt at the time without reliving the situation
      emotionally.
4.  Name the signature lightly.
    → Use simple descriptors (tight, urgent, buzzy, foggy, heavy) to label the
      bodily or perceptual quality you notice.
5.  Pause.
    → Notice how recognition alone changes your relationship to the memory.

### What to Watch For

> sensations of tightening, compression, or constriction
> a sense of urgency or pressure to reach a conclusion
> thought moving faster than bodily sensing
> imagery or meaning becoming dramatic or inflated
> loss of neutrality or steadiness
> a feeling of being pulled toward interpretation rather than present

**Reflection**

- ↺ What bodily or perceptual signal let you know distortion was occurring?
- ↺ Did the distortion have a recognizable texture or quality?
- ↺ Which distortion pattern felt most familiar or recurring?
- ↺ How early in the process could you recognize it?
- ↺ What might have shifted if you had paused at that moment?

*What you're noticing.*

## EXPLORATION 15.2: Signal vs. Interference Scan

Clarity Amid Competing Impressions

### Objective

To distinguish between clear, steady signal and impressions influenced by emotional charge or urgency by attending to their qualitative differences.

Your system already detects these shifts. This practice makes them more visible.

### Setup

Sit in a supported position. Pause for 15–30 seconds and let your breath find its natural rhythm.

### Steps

1. Allow an impression to arise.
   → Do not search or choose.
   → Let something register on its own.
2. Notice its qualitative character.
3. Without interpreting meaning, ask:
   → Does this feel neutral and steady?
     (may indicate perceptual coherence)
   → Does this feel emotionally charged?
     (may reflect emotional overlay)
   → Does this feel pressured, insistent, or demanding?
     (may indicate distortion or interference)
4. Pause rather than decide.
5. Let the impression remain without acting on it.
6. Notice the effect on your system.
7. Observe whether your attention settles or activates as you stay with it.

### What to Watch For

〉 impressions that feel steadier or less demanding
〉 impressions that feel charged, urgent, or mentally loud
〉 differences in how easily your body remains settled
〉 whether the impression invites patience or pushes for conclusion

## Reflection

- ↻ How did a steadier impression differ from one that felt charged or pressured?
- ↻ What did you notice in your body as you stayed with each?
- ↻ Did one quality allow your system to settle more easily?
- ↻ What shifted when you stopped trying to interpret the impression?
- ↻ Which quality (steadiness, neutrality, or lack of urgency) felt most reliable for you?

*What you're noticing.*

# EXPLORATION 15.3: Belief Interference

Belief & Perceptual Filtering

## Objective

To notice how expectation influences what becomes visible within what you perceive.

## Setup

Sit in a supported position. Allow your breathing to become steady and natural.

## Steps

1. Recall a recent situation where your interpretation felt immediate or certain.
2. Bring the situation lightly to mind.
3. Notice the interpretation that formed first.
4. Ask: *What belief or assumption may have shaped this interpretation?*
5. Without forcing an answer, allow the situation to reorganize.
6. Ask a second question: *What else might have been present that I did not notice initially?*
7. Hold the experience briefly without replacing the interpretation with a new one.

## What to Watch For

> new details appearing
> earlier certainty softening
> multiple interpretations becoming possible
> signals that were previously overlooked

## Reflection

↺ Did your interpretation shift once your belief was questioned?
↺ What changed when the interpretation was held more lightly?
↺ Did additional information become noticeable?

*What you're noticing.*

## EXPLORATION 15.4: Boundary Reset After Connection

Re-orienting Attention After Interaction

### Objective

To restore clarity by disengaging your attention from residual relational influence after interpersonal or environmental contact.

### Setup

This can be done seated, standing, or while walking (ideally shortly after an interaction).

### Steps

1. Pause and orient your attention inward.
   - → Bring your attention to your body and immediate physical presence.
2. Notice residual influence.
   - → Without judgment, notice whether any sensations, emotions, images, or impressions remain that seem connected to the recent interaction.
3. Gather your attention.
   - → On an exhale, allow your attention to return toward your own body: breath, posture, weight, or connection with the ground.
4. Re-establish your baseline.
   - → Let your attention move into what feels like your current state, without trying to remove anything.
5. Pause and notice.
   - → Allow a few seconds for your attention to stabilize before moving on.

### What to Watch For

- ⟩ sensations or impressions that fade as your attention re-centers
- ⟩ your emotional tone becoming quieter or more neutral
- ⟩ your thoughts or imagery losing intensity when not engaged
- ⟩ a sense of internal steadiness or privacy returning
- ⟩ a more defined differentiation between your own state and what was picked up relationally
- ⟩ clarity returning as absence of interference, not as new information

**Reflection**

- ↺ What shifted when you gathered your attention back to your own body?
- ↺ Did any sensations, emotions, or impressions release or fade?
- ↺ How did your internal state differ before and after re-orienting?
- ↺ Did clarity return gradually or all at once?
- ↺ What does "being back in yourself" feel like for you?

*What you're noticing.*

**INTEGRATION PRACTICE 15**
## The Clearest Possible State

Before engaging broader perceptual awareness, take a moment to establish the clearest available baseline:

1. **Ground your body.** Notice connection, weight, and physical presence.
2. **Center your attention.** Let your attention gather naturally rather than spread outward.
3. **Re-establish boundaries of attention.** Allow your attention to rest primarily within your own body and immediate experience.
4. **Enter perceptual coherence.** Let your breath, body, and attention form into a steady, regulated state.
5. **Notice from here.** Permit what you notice to shape without effort or expectation.

If distortion appears:

1. **Pause.** Stop interpreting or acting.
2. **Re-orient.** Return your attention to body, breath, and baseline.
3. **Resume.** Continue only if clarity returns on its own.

Clarity is not forced. It is restored by returning to orientation.

*Observations.*

**Closing Thought**

Distortion is not a flaw in you. It is part of the landscape of perception.

The aim is not perfect purity. It is perceptual maturity.

You now have discovered:

> why distortion happens
> how it registers
> how to recognize it
> how to respond to it
> how to return to clarity

The next chapter turns to timeline sensitivity: how awareness can move across past, present, and emerging patterns while you, as the perceiver, remains steady, without dramatizing, merging, or fragmenting.

# 16 I Timeline Sensitivity
## How Time Registers

**Opening Invitation**

Timeline sensitivity is not fortune-telling.

It is not prophecy.

It is not watching a movie of the future.

It is the noticing of temporal movement as it begins to organize, before it becomes fully visible.

Time does not arrive all at once.

Events accumulate. → Emotional tone gathers. → Decisions build direction. → Internal states shift before behavior changes.

You may already recognize it:

> sensing when someone is about to call
> feeling a relationship shift before it becomes explicit
> noticing a bodily "drop" before difficult news
> detecting a change in atmosphere before someone speaks
> knowing not to go somewhere and later understanding why

These are not dramatic abilities. They reflect pattern recognition across time.

Your system detects micro-shifts in tone, rhythm, posture, language, and context long before they assemble into visible outcomes.

Timeline sensitivity is not about predicting events, but rather it is about detecting trajectory.

Trajectory is the direction in which a pattern is moving. It is momentum before manifestation.

Timeline sensitivity does not tell you what will happen. Instead, it helps you recognize what is already unfolding.

It is not something to acquire.

It is something to notice, refine, and interpret without distortion.

**Note on Anxiety & Projection**

Timeline sensitivity can be confused with anxiety or projection.

Anxiety amplifies imagined outcomes and attaches urgency to them. Projection fills uncertainty with narrative.

Both introduce emotional charge and premature certainty.

Timeline sensitivity, by contrast, is more neutral. It detects directional change without insisting on a specific conclusion. It feels like orientation rather than alarm: a subtle shift in tone, coherence, or momentum rather than a dramatic story about what will happen.

If the experience feels urgent, catastrophic, or emotionally charged, it is likely anxiety.

If it feels steady, directional, and proportionate, it is likely sensitivity to trajectory.

*Pause. Check resonance.*

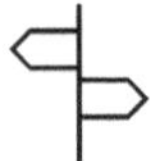

## How Time Registers in Lived Perception

**Perceiving Time in Motion**

Time is not experienced only as clock-time. In lived perception it appears as movement: intention forming, probability shifting, momentum gathering within the present.

Three practical observations:

1. Events generate precursors before they become visible.
2. Trajectories leave traces, slight shifts in mood, body, and context.
3. Your system detects these shifts before the intellect explains them.

Time is first experienced phenomenologically, through body, attention, and awareness. It is not encountered as calendar units or measured intervals, but as change:

> shifts in tone
> tension
> pacing
> direction readiness

You feel time before you think about it.

A pause lengthens when tension builds. → Momentum accelerates when direction gathers. → Something unresolved can feel imminent before any visible event confirms it.

Your body senses acceleration, hesitation, or settling before narrative forms around it.

Phenomenological time is lived time: the felt experience of unfolding from within.

Timeline sensitivity begins there, not in prediction, but in recognizing momentum as it accumulates across experience.

You are not seeing the future; you are noticing the direction a pattern is already taking.

Ingo sometimes referred to this as *future memory*... not memory of a fixed outcome, but recognition of a trajectory already forming.

For clarity here, we will keep the language simple:

**Timeline sensitivity is noticing what is approaching as it begins to organize.**

Pause. Check resonance.

Pause. Check resonance.

## Differentiating Timeline Sensitivity from Imagination, Anxiety, & Projection

Timeline sensitivity can be confused with two different distortions: story and urgency.

Imagination and projection distort through narrative construction. They generate content, filling uncertainty with images, explanations, and dramatic sequence.

Anxiety distorts through urgency. It compresses time, amplifies threat, and demands immediate conclusion.

Timeline sensitivity does neither.

> It does not build elaborate story.
> It does not accelerate into alarm.

Instead, it detects directional movement without insisting on interpretation.

A useful distinction:

> When story increases, you are likely in imagination or projection.
> When urgency increases, you are likely in anxiety.
> When steadiness increases, you are likely perceiving trajectory.

Imagination elaborates, anxiety accelerates, while timeline sensitivity orients.

Timeline signals tend to be neutral, not emotionally amplified, not narratively dense. They are often brief, proportionate, and easy to overlook.

Rather than increasing reactivity, they tend to reduce it.

What they increase is not certainty, but responsibility.


## How the Future Communicates

Timeline signals tend to appear in three primary forms:

1. Physiological pre-reaction: Your perceptual awareness system shifts before you know why (a subtle tightening, drop, pull, or change in baseline tone).
2. Contextual shift: A change in density, pressure, openness, constriction, rise, drop, or gentle "weight" in your immediate experience.
3. Symbolic fragments: Images, metaphors, textures, or impressions that convey direction and quality rather than literal scenes.

These signals are often faint.

If you expect drama, you will overlook them.

## Two Principles That Keep This Clean

First: The future is not fixed. It's probabilistic. Your system doesn't register every possible outcome. It registers what is becoming most likely... the strongest current in motion. Second: Timeline signals arrive in tiers.

**Tier 1:** Pre-sensory activation. Your body reacts before meaning forms. This is the earliest timeline signal. Before thoughts, imagery, or emotion arise, your nervous system shifts.

Common markers may include:

> tightening in your chest
> a drop or hollowing in your stomach
> a sudden breath change
> temperature shifts (cooling, warmth, chills)
> heightened alertness
> a sense that the air has become denser or thinner

At this stage, there is no story. Only a physiological adjustment to something not yet present. This tier is easy to miss because it happens quickly and because your intellect tends to rush ahead to explanation.

**Tier 2:** Pre-emotional resonance. An emotion appears before its apparent cause.

In this stage, emotional tone arrives slightly ahead of the event or interaction that later explains it. The feeling may seem out of place in the moment, only to make sense when circumstances unfold.

Unlike Tier 1, where the signal appears primarily as physiological change, Tier 2 organizes as emotional tone. Your system begins registering relational or situational direction before your intellect identifies what is occurring.

Common markers may include:

> sudden unease in an otherwise neutral moment
> a quiet sense of anticipation without clear reason
> warmth or ease toward someone before interaction develops
> tension or hesitation before conflict becomes visible
> sadness or concern before news or change becomes known

**Tier 3:** Symbolic translation. Your intellect renders the approach into symbols:

> images / metaphors
> textures / colors / shapes
> fragments of meaning

This is not literal. It's directional. This is the territory Ingo explored when describing what he called our innate "Nostradamus Factor": your system's sensitivity to emerging trajectories rather than fixed outcomes.





*Pause. Check resonance.*

## Why Timeline Signals Are Often Misread

Four common reasons:

1.  Fear and desire: strong emotion distorts faster than anything else.
2.  Symbol literalism: metaphors get treated as facts.
3.  Narrative inflation: a faint signal becomes a full story.
4.  Boundary confusion: you sense someone else's trajectory and assume it's
    yours.

When timeline sensitivity feels unreliable, it's usually interpretation, not sensing,
that's unstable.

> *Pause. Check resonance.*

## The Timeline Sensitivity Scale

A simple way to notice the intensity of timeline sensitivity is by tracking how its signals appear.

This scale offers a practical way to map those shifts as they move from subtle registration toward clearer recognition.

### Level 1: Whisper

A slight change in tone or atmosphere. Something feels different, but the shift is so subtle it could easily be overlooked.

### Level 2: Pull

Your attention leans toward or away from something without clear explanation. Your focus shifts before you consciously decide why.

### Level 3: Pressure

Your body reacts physically. Sensations such as tightening, heaviness, alertness, or breath change signal that your system has registered something significant.

### Level 4: Symbolic burst

An image, metaphor, or sensory-like impression appears. The information arrives in compressed symbolic form rather than through direct sensory cues.

### Level 5: Clarity

A calm, grounded knowing appears without urgency or emotional charge. The signal feels steady rather than dramatic.

### Level 6: Emotional resonance

An emotion arises that does not match the present moment. Later it becomes clear that the feeling corresponded to what unfolded. Emotional resonance often appears when earlier, subtler signals were not consciously noticed.

### Level 7: Impact

The event occurs and the earlier signals become recognizable in retrospect. The pattern becomes clear because the outcome has now appeared.

Higher levels are not more accurate. They simply reflect stronger registration or later recognition within the same unfolding pattern.

The scale is not meant for dramatization. It exists to help you track signals without dismissing them, and without inflating them.

*Pause. Check resonance.*

**The Five Pathways of Timeline Signals**

Timeline signals tend to register through five channels:

Physical (pre-sensory reactions):

> tightness
> chills
> warmth
> sudden stillness

Emotional (pre-emotional activation):

> dread
> anticipation
> sadness
> relief

Cognitive (sudden knowing/directive clarity):

> "call them"
> "don't go"
> "this is shifting"

Symbolic (images or metaphors):

> waves
> doors
> storms
> breaking
> opening
> dimming

Environmental and Relational Tone (energetic shifts):

> expansion
> contraction
> magnetism
> dullness
> brightness
> pressure

These channels can help you recognize all five without inflating or dramatizing them.

*Pause. Check resonance.*

*Pause. Check resonance.*

## EXPLORATION 16.1: The Pre-Sensory Scan

Direction Before Thought

### Objective

To notice subtle physiological shifts that arise before thought, emotion, or narrative forms.

### Setup

Adopt a quiet posture. Let your breath move without adjustment.

### Steps

1. Bring to mind someone or something you are genuinely connected to (a person, decision, project, or upcoming situation).
2. Notice small changes in your:
   - → chest
   - → belly
   - → spine
   - → overall sense of bodily orientation or presence
3. Pay attention to sensations that appear before explanations or stories begin to form. These are early timeline signals registered through the body.

### What to Watch For

> your breath catching or deepening slightly
> a tightening, softening, drop, or lift
> warmth or coolness
> a brief internal pause
> a shift in how present or open your body feels

### Reflection

↺ What appeared first: sensation, emotion, thought, or image?
↺ Did the signal feel neutral, pressured, or emotionally charged?
↺ Where in your system do you notice early shifts most consistently?

*What you're noticing.*

*What you're noticing.*

## EXPLORATION 16.2: The Probability Compass
Direction Without Forcing Outcome

### Objective

To notice directional momentum (such as opening or closing) without converting it into prediction or conclusion.

### Setup

Be still for a moment. Allow your breath to even out naturally.

### Steps

1. Bring to mind a specific situation you are currently engaged with (a decision, relationship, project, or unfolding circumstance).
2. Ask, without pressure: *Does this feel more open, more closed, or indeterminate right now?*
3. Notice subtle indicators such as:
   - → whether your sense of bodily orientation expands, contracts, or remains steady
   - → whether your posture inclines forward, back, or stays neutral
4. Record the directional impression only, without adding explanation or story. This is how probability tends to register: as orientation, not outcome.

### What to Watch For

- ⟩ a sense of opening or increased possibility
- ⟩ a sense of closing or reduced movement
- ⟩ momentum, or an inclination toward pause or withdrawal
- ⟩ neutrality or lack of directional signal

### Reflection

- ↺ Which cue was clearest for you: bodily orientation, posture, breath, or overall tone?
- ↺ Did you notice any urge to turn direction into certainty or narrative?
- ↺ How does it feel to acknowledge direction without needing an answer?

*What you're noticing.*

*What you're noticing.*

**EXPLORATION 16.3: Symbolic Reading**
Working with Symbolic Timeline Signals Without Taking Them Literally

## Objective

To notice symbolic impressions as expressions of quality and movement, without treating them as literal future scenes or outcomes.

## Setup

Sit in a stable posture. Allow your breath to find its own rhythm.

## Steps

1. Allow a symbolic impression to arise in relation to a situation (this may appear as an image, texture, movement, atmosphere, or fragment).
2. Record the impression exactly as it appeared, without explanation or interpretation.
3. Inquire:
   → What quality does this symbol seem to carry?
   → What movement is suggested (such as opening, closing, rising, breaking, dispersing, pausing)?
   → What kind of change, if any, does it seem to reflect (beginning, ending, intensifying, softening)?
4. Stay with qualities and movement rather than translating the symbol into events or conclusions.

## What to Watch For

⟩ symbols seeming to shift or simplify when not treated literally
⟩ emotional charge rising or falling as attention changes
⟩ some impressions presenting as simple or directional rather than detailed

## Reflection

↺ What changed when you related to the symbol as movement rather than prediction?
↺ Did the impression feel neutral, emotionally charged, or unclear?
↺ What became visible when you stayed with quality instead of story?

## EXPLORATION 16.4: Timeline Boundary Check
Checking Whether an Impression Is Yours

### Objective

To notice whether an impression feels personally grounded, externally influenced, or simply transient, without forcing a conclusion.

### Setup

Establish a steady posture. Let your breathing remain unforced.

### Steps

1. Notice your baseline state before bringing anything to mind.
2. Sense your posture, breathing, and emotional tone as they are right now.
3. Bring the impression into your awareness (this might be a sensation, symbolic fragment, directive clarity, or emotional tone).
4. Ask: *How does this relate to my system right now?*
5. Notice any shift in the impression as you ask:
    - → Does it seem to settle, move, or change quality?
    - → Does it draw closer to bodily awareness, drift outward, or fade?
6. Stay with what changes rather than deciding what the impression "is."

### What to Watch For

> impressions that feel personally relevant settling or organizing themselves
> impressions that are not personally relevant loosening, drifting, or lifting away
> some impressions dissolving when attention becomes neutral
> clarity sometimes appearing as absence of pull rather than new information

### Reflection

↺ What changed when you questioned the impression's relationship to you?
↺ How did impressions that felt personally grounded differ from those that did not?
↺ What cues were most informative for you: bodily sensation, emotional tone, or the impression's stability over time?

**Integration Practice 16**
**The Timeline Journal**

Each day, note any of the following that stand out:

**Pre-sensory reactions.** Bodily shifts that appear without an immediate explanation.

**Pre-emotional resonance.** Emotional tone that arrives before there is an obvious cause.

**Symbolic fragments.** Images, metaphors, textures, or impressions that linger.

**Directive clarity.** Simple orientations such as call, pause, wait, or don't go, without reasoning attached.

**Contextual or relational shifts.** Changes in openness, contraction, pressure, brightness, or dullness in your overall sense of the situation.

Later (without judgment or self-evaluation) notice how these entries relate to what unfolded over time. This practice supports calibration rather than confirmation: discovering how your system detects shifts in timing and direction, and how those early impressions evolve.

*Observations.*

**Closing Thought**

The future does not conceal itself.

It signals through body, emotion, context, and symbol.

The earlier a signal appears, the quieter it tends to be.

The quieter it is, the less it has been shaped by reaction, interpretation, or narrative.

As you become able to recognize:

> pre-sensory activation
> pre-emotional resonance
> symbolic fragments
> contextual shifts
> directional momentum...

...you may begin to see that timeline sensitivity is not "seeing the future."

It is detecting trajectory before it becomes visible.

Timeline sensitivity provides directional information before your intellect organizes it into explanation.

What follows matters.

> Information can be steadied or dramatized.
> It can be clarified or overlaid.
> It can remain directional or harden into premature meaning.

In the next chapter, we turn to meaning-making: how to extract understanding from complex impressions without distortion, urgency, or narrative overlay.

# 17 | Signal Interpretation & Meaning-Making
## Letting Meaning Form Without Distortion

### Opening Invitation

By now, you've explored how information registers across multiple channels: bodily, emotional, relational, symbolic, and temporal.

But being aware alone is not enough.

The moment you search for meaning, interpretation begins, and this is where clarity is most often lost.

Interpretation is where:

⟩ bias enters
⟩ emotion colors meaning
⟩ symbols are taken literally
⟩ anticipatory perception collapses into fantasy
⟩ empathy blurs into entanglement
⟩ clarity turns into confusion

This chapter focuses on how meaning forms, and how to experience that process without collapsing into story or projection.

Meaning-making is not automatic.

It develops through discernment.

As it stabilizes, information becomes more trustworthy.

Anyone familiar with a radio knows the sound of static.

When a signal is clear, meaning comes through cleanly. When interference enters, the message distorts.

Interpretation works the same way.

By the time you ask, "What does this mean?" you are no longer receiving. You are filtering.

And this is where clarity is most often lost.

— Adapted from Ingo Swann, *The "Noisy Mind/Dirty Data" Issue*

*What you're noticing.*

## The Three Stages of Interpretation

Every impression, no matter how complex, moves through three functional stages:

1. **Signal.** The raw information as it is detected.
2. **Symbol.** How your intellect represents that registration.
3. **Story.** How your intellect interprets what it thinks the symbol means.

## A Simple Illustration

Imagine encountering the symbol of a labyrinth.

At first, it is only a signal: a pattern of lines.

Soon it becomes a symbol: a maze, a path, a design.

Then the story begins.

You may think of being lost, searching for an exit, or finding a hidden center.

But the labyrinth itself has not changed.

Only the meaning applied to it has expanded.

This is how interpretation works.

---

*Consider this before beginning the material that follows.*

**Stage 1: The SIGNAL**

What is registered through organismic perception.

The signal is the initial registration before interpretation. It may appear as:

> sensation
> texture
> temperature
> pressure
> direction
> movement
> tone
> subtle emotional resonance
> symbolic fragments
> pre-sensory activation

Signal is the primary or raw data.

Some examples:

> a sudden sharpness in the space around you
> a sinking in the stomach
> a pressure change in the room
> a symbolic image that appears quietly, without emotional charge
> a gentle "pull" toward or away from something
> a calm, non-urgent certainty

This is the stage from which interpretation is most stable.

The signal is usually:

> small
> quiet
> subtle
> relatively neutral

The signal does not argue, persuade, or insist. It simply registers.

When an impression becomes loud, emotionally charged, dramatic, or urgent, you are usually no longer in the signal. You are in **Stage 3: Story**.

## Stage 2: The SYMBOL

The intellect's attempt to represent the signal.

When you receive a signal your intellect cannot easily name, it often translates it into a symbol.

Symbols may appear as:

> images
> metaphors
> shapes
> colors
> sensations
> scenes
> archetypal figures
> fragments of memory
> dreamlike impressions

This is the comparator system at work: translating the unknown into something familiar enough to handle.

A symbol is not the meaning itself.

A symbol points toward meaning.

For example, in some people's experience, a symbol might appear as:

> waves → a sense of fluctuation or changing intensity
> broken glass → a sense of fragility or something no longer intact
> lightning → a sense of suddenness or high-intensity shift
> a cold wind → a sense of distance or separation
> thick air → a sense of heaviness or stuckness
> a door → a sense of threshold or change in possibility

These are not fixed definitions.

They illustrate how symbols can express movement and tone rather than literal scenes or predictions.

**Stage 3: The STORY**

Your intellect's interpretation.

This is where the process most often goes off track.

The story includes:

> narrative
> explanations
> fears
> desires
> assumptions
> personal history
> projection
> dramatic meaning

The story is not the signal. It is what your intellect thinks the signal (and its symbols) mean.

Story-making is natural. Your intellect is designed to organize information into explanation. Difficulty arises only when story forms faster than observation.

Your work is to:

1. separate story from symbol, and
2. separate symbol from signal...

...so that meaning forms gradually, with less distortion and less urgency.

## The Golden Rule of Interpretation

Stay as close to the signal as possible.

The closer your attention remains to raw data, the less interpretation is shaped by assumption, emotion, or story.

## The Four Pillars of Clean Interpretation

Rather than rules, these function as orienting supports. They help meaning form without being forced:

**1. Sensation First.** Begin with what was registered before understanding began.

You might ask:

⟩ Where in your body or immediate awareness did this register?
⟩ What was the basic tone (for example: sharp or soft, heavy, or light)?
⟩ Was there a sense of direction (toward, away, expanding, contracting)?
⟩ What, if anything, shifted in your overall sense of the situation?

Staying close to sensation helps keep interpretation grounded.

**2. Symbol as Metaphor.** Treat symbols as representations rather than otatomonto.

Symbols often reflect:

⟩ movement
⟩ pattern
⟩ emotional tone
⟩ trajectory

They are best approached as metaphors for how something is moving, not as literal depictions.

**3. Emotion as Indicator, Not Explanation.** Emotion within what is being perceived can offer information without defining meaning.

Emotion may reflect:

⟩ resonance ("this touches me")
⟩ alignment with a developing situation
⟩ entanglement or personal activation

Emotion is not meaning itself.

It is the touch point regarding how information is interacting with your system.

**4. Intellect Last.** Allow reasoning to enter only after signal and symbol have been clarified.

When your intellect does engage, it helps to ask:

> What is the simplest way to describe what changed?
> What movement is present, independent of storyline?
> What was added only after interpretation began?

Often, simplicity preserves clarity better than complexity.

*Pause. Check resonance.*

## Common Movements Underlying Signals

Across many experiences, your system often seems to organize around a small number of basic directional movements:

> toward
> away
> upward or expanding
> downward or contracting

Symbols frequently express one or more of these movements in visual or sensory form.

For example, some people may notice associations such as:

> lightning → sudden upward or activating movement
> shadow → downward or withdrawing movement
> waves → rhythmic toward/away movement
> an open door → expansion or entry
> a closed door → contraction or pause

These are not fixed meanings. They illustrate how symbols can point to movement and tone, rather than events.

*Pause. Check resonance.*

*What you're noticing.*

## Working with Symbolic Impressions

When symbolic impressions appear, the task is not to decode them immediately or search for a fixed meaning. Symbols are simply one way your system renders complex information. Before interpretation begins, it can help to notice how the impression formed.

A simple orientation is:

1. Identify the signal: the raw shift that first registered (sensation, tone, direction, pressure).
2. Notice the symbolic form: the image, metaphor, or fragment your mind used to represent that registration.
3. Notice the quality or pattern the symbol carries (movement, tone, density, expansion, contraction).
4. Observe how the impression changes as attention rests on it.
5. Allow meaning to organize gradually rather than forcing a conclusion.

Meaning often clarifies through stability and repetition rather than immediate interpretation.

*Pause. Check resonance.*

**A Way to Approach Meaning Without Guessing**

Rather than a formula, this is a sequence of attention.

1. **Notice the signal.** What was actually registered? (sensation, texture, tone, directional shift)
2. **Notice the movement.** Did it feel more toward, away, expanding, or contracting?
3. **Notice the tone.** For example: warm or cool, light, or heavy, calm or sharp.
4. **Notice whether a symbol appeared.** What image, metaphor, or fragment appeared, if any?
5. **Hold a neutral translation.** Describe the symbol in terms of movement and tone, without story. Only then allow interpretation. Ask: *What understanding fits the signal without adding drama or certainty?*


**Illustrative Examples (Not Templates)**

These examples are offered to show process, not to define meaning. What matters is not the conclusion, but how it forms.

**Example 1**

⟩ Signal: lightness in the chest
⟩ Symbol: a white bird
⟩ Movement: upward / expanding
⟩ Tone: light, quiet
⟩ Possible understanding: a sense of release, openness, or easing may be present

**Example 2**

⟩ Signal: contraction and sharpness
⟩ Symbol: broken glass
⟩ Movement: downward / fragmenting
⟩ Tone: abrupt
⟩ Possible understanding: a sense of disruption, breach, or loss of coherence

**Example 3**

⟩ Signal: warmth spreading
⟩ Symbol: sunlight
⟩ Movement: upward / expanding
⟩ Tone: steady
⟩ Possible understanding: strengthening clarity or connection

Pause. Check resonance.

Pause. Check resonance.

Common Sources of Interpretation Drift

> **Rushing meaning**
  → Stay with sensation a little longer before naming anything.
> **Taking symbols literally**
  → Translate movement and tone rather than image.
> **Blending emotion with meaning**
  → Separate current emotional state from perceptual tone.
> **Assuming the signal refers outward**
  → Gently check whether it relates to you, another, or context.
> **Letting fear or desire lead**
  → Re-enter grounded awareness before interpreting.
> **Overcomplicating**
  → Return to the simplest description of movement and tone.

*Pause. Check resonance.*

## EXPLORATION 17.1: The Signal Extraction Drill

Separating the Signal from the Story

### Objective

To practice letting meaning form through sensation, movement, and tone rather than from story or assumption.

### Setup

Sit in a stable, supported position. Let your breath move without adjustment.

### Steps

1. Choose a recent impression (this may be a dream image, a spontaneous symbol, or a "weird feeling" that lingered).
2. Write down, in order:
   - → Signal: what was registered before explanation (sensation, texture, pressure, direction).
   - → Symbol: any image, metaphor, or fragment that appeared.
   - → Movement: for example: toward, away, upward, downward, expanding, contracting.
   - → Tone: for example: warm, cool, light, heavy, calm, sharp.
   - → Provisional understanding: one simple sentence describing movement and quality, without narrative.
3. Keep each entry brief. Do not elaborate.

### What to Watch For

⟩ how quickly your intellect wants to jump ahead to explanation
⟩ a signal often feels simpler or quieter than the symbol, that understanding sometimes clarifies when reduced to a single, restrained sentence

### Reflection

↺ Which part of the process required the most restraint: staying with raw sensation, naming movement, or limiting story?
↺ Did the final understanding feel quieter or less dramatic than your usual interpretations?
↺ What changed in emotional charge once the impression was reduced to signal and movement?

# EXPLORATION 17.2: The Two-Signal Comparison
Your Personal Interpretation Tendencies

## Objective

To notice differences in how impressions register when perception feels evident versus when interpretation becomes strained or distorted, allowing your own patterns to become visible over time.

## Setup

Settle into a quiet position and let your breathing proceed without control.

## Steps

1. Bring to mind two past impressions:
   - → one that later felt clear, settled, or coherent
   - → one that felt confusing, unstable, or off
2. For each impression, note:
   - → bodily sensation (location, steadiness, contraction, or ease)
   - → symbol tone (simple, complex, dramatic, neutral, absent)
   - → emotional intensity (low, moderate, high, shifting)
   - → sense of movement (toward, away, expanding, contracting, unclear)
3. Compare the two impressions without judging either one.
4. Look for recurring differences rather than conclusions.

## What to Watch For

> impressions that felt clearer registering with less urgency or drama
> impressions that felt confusing carrying stronger emotional charge
> symbols feeling simpler or quieter in clearer impressions
> interpretation accelerating more quickly in impressions that later felt off

## Reflection

↺ What differences stood out most clearly between the two impressions?
↺ Were there consistent cues that appeared before confusion or distortion set in?
↺ How early might those cues have been noticed if your attention had slowed?

**EXPLORATION 17.3: Symbol Deconstruction**
Attending to Signal, Movement, & Quality

## Objective

To explore how symbolic impressions reorganize when your attention rests on movement and quality rather than literal imagery.

## Setup

Sit in a stable posture. Allow your breathing to remain unforced. Let your attention soften without searching for imagery.

## Steps

1. If no symbolic impression is immediately present, recall one that recently lingered (from a dream, a spontaneous image, or a moment of recognition).
   → Allow its outline to return without trying to recreate it vividly.
2. When a symbolic impression is present, pause before interpreting it.
   → This may appear as a bodily shift, tone, pressure, or subtle orientation.
3. Note the following qualities of the impression:
   → Movement: rising, falling, opening, closing, circling, dispersing, colliding.
   → Tone: calm, tense, hopeful, unsettled, neutral.
   → Qualitative texture: sharp or soft, bright, or dim, heavy or light.
4. Set aside the literal content of the symbol (such as "bird," "storm," or "building") and stay with movement, tone, and texture alone.
5. Allow the impression to remain present without explanation or narrative.

## What to Watch For

> shifts in intensity when literal content is set aside
> movement and tone carrying more information than imagery
> parts of the symbol losing urgency or authority when narrative is suspended
> meaning remaining present even as story drops away

## Reflection

↺ What changed when you focused on signal, movement, and quality rather than imagery?
↺ Did the symbol feel easier to hold without becoming literal?
↺ What kind of information remained when narrative was suspended?

*What you're noticing.*

*What you're noticing.*

**Integration Practice 17**
**Meaning Without Story**

As a brief, ongoing practice:

1.  When a perception arises:
    - → stay with it at the level of signal
    - → notice movement
    - → notice tone
    - → notice whether a symbolic image or fragment appears
2.  Allow any simple understanding to form, if it does.
3.  Pause before building an explanation or narrative.
4.  Nothing needs to be concluded.

This practice supports perceptual coherence by letting understanding remain close to organismic perception, without adding unnecessary story.

*Observations.*

**Closing Thought**

Meaning-making is not guessing.

It is not imagining.

It is not storytelling.

In this context, meaning-making involves:

> staying close to the signal
> allowing symbols to remain symbolic
> attending to movement rather than imagery
> noticing tone rather than narrative
> letting your intellect enter late rather than lead

When interpretation remains close to the signal, understanding tends to become:

> more differentiated
> more defined
> less reactive
> more stable over time

As what you notice enlarges, interpretation must become more disciplined.

That discipline is not restriction. It is what allows complexity to be held without collapse.

You are now prepared to move into what is next: navigating multiple perceptual contexts at once (personal, relational, environmental, and symbolic) while remaining grounded, coherent, and centered.

# CODA

# WHEN PERCEPTION BECOMES DISCERNMENT

## Opening Invitation

You did not move through this book by trying to change perception.

You moved through it by discovering how perception already organizes.

Along the way, you've experienced how:

> perception does not arrive through a single channel
> clarity depends more on differentiation than intensity
> symbolic experience is compression, not fantasy
> distortion is predictable, textured, and correctable
> meaning becomes cleaner when it forms slowly
> steadiness matters more than reach

You have not been asked to believe anything new.

You have been asked to notice more precisely.

What makes information trustworthy at this level is not expansion. It is discernment.

## What You Have Already Integrated

Across these chapters you have:

> **Differentiated perceptual pathways.**
> You explored how to recognize whether information arrived literally, inferentially, or symbolically, before deciding what to do with it.

> **Developed symbolic literacy.**
> You mapped out how symbolic cognition functions, why it exists, and how to work with symbols without collapsing into story, prediction, or belief.

> **Recognized distortion as process, not failure.**
> You delved into how emotional charge, cognitive overlay, comparator inflation, boundary weakening, and fatigue alter perception, and how quickly clarity returns once they are noticed.

> **Refined timeline sensitivity.**
> You discovered how to recognize the early registration of movement and probability, rather than mistaking it for prophecy or fixed outcome.

> **Disciplined interpretation.**
> You navigated through how to let meaning form from signal → symbol → understanding, rather than leaping into narrative.

This is not about more information. It is about greater differentiation.

## Why Discernment Is Not the End

As what you become aware of becomes more differentiated, something subtle happens.

You may notice:

> impressions arriving earlier and in subtler form
> meaning forming without urgency
> symbolic material feeling less dramatic
> anticipatory signals registering without anxiety
> less need to decide what something "is"

This is not completion.

It is preparation.

Because once the process becomes cleaner, a new challenge appears:

1. How do you live inside multiple perceptual contexts at once?
2. How do you stay oriented while switching frames?
3. How do you remain ethical, grounded, and relational while sensing broadly?
4. How do you act responsibly with information that is incomplete, probabilistic, or symbolic?

At this stage, clarity alone is not sufficient.

What becomes essential is a stable vantage point within your awareness, one that can register sensation, emotion, symbol, and meaning without being pulled into any of them.

Discernment makes what you perceive reliable.

Orientation makes it livable. Integration makes it usable.


## The Pivot into Book Four

Book Three asked:

*How does meaning take shape, and what alters its form?*

What comes next asks:

*How do I live inside this awareness without fragmenting, inflating, or withdrawing from ordinary life?*

The experiences ahead is not about more depth.

They are about integration across contexts.

You will move into:

> navigating multiple reference frames at once
> maintaining coherence as perception widens
> acting without over-identifying with what you sense
> staying human, relational, and grounded
> letting perception inform action without overruling judgment

This is where perception stops being something you have and becomes something you live from.

## Closing Thought

You are no longer working to sense more. You are working to remain oriented.

You now know that:

> clarity does not rush
> meaningful perception is often neutral
> symbols do not need interpretation to be useful
> anticipation does not require prediction
> steadiness matters more than certainty

You do not need to force insight.

You do not need to explain everything you sense.

You do not need to collapse meaning into story.

What you perceive becomes most accurate when it is allowed to remain partial, quiet, and well-held.

What comes next is not about expanding beyond yourself.

It is about moving through the world with your organismic intelligence online, without losing humility or discernment.

Book Three ends here:

> Not because the work is complete .
> But because your foundation is now stable enough to carry what follows.

# APPENDIX

## Quick Reset Practices

The brief resets below are not techniques to master or practices to perform regularly. They are simple ways of returning your system to a workable state when it drifts, intensifies, or becomes unclear.

You may use them as needed, or not at all.

### Body Reset
### (returning to physical presence)

〉 Exhale longer than you inhale.
〉 Relax your shoulders.
〉 Feel a connection to the ground through your feet or seat.
〉 Drop into the present moment.

### Boundary Reset
### (restoring perceptual containment)

〉 Inhale → gently gather your attention to your perimeter.
〉 Exhale → allow your boundary to close.
〉 Focus on a soft containment around the body.

### Coherence Reset
### (stabilizing rhythm and tone)

〉 Inhale for 5 seconds.
〉 Exhale for 5 seconds.
〉 Bring to mind something you appreciate.
〉 Let your attention smooth and stabilize.

### Emotional Check-In
### (staying oriented with feeling)

〉 Where is the sensation located?
〉 What is its texture?
〉 What is its direction (up / down / inward / outward)?
〉 Can it soften with one breath?

### Perceptual Reorientation
### (returning to balanced attention)

〉 Turn your attention inward.
〉 Soften your visual focus.
〉 Allow your awareness to include the room around you.

# SELECTED SCIENTIFIC & PHILOSOPHICAL FOUNDATIONS

The following works have informed the biological, cognitive, and phenomenological perspectives that shape this book.

They are not cited exhaustively, but represent foundational contributions in predictive processing, interoception, non-conscious perception, symbolic cognition, pattern recognition, attentional selection, and meaning-making.

The explorations in this book draw upon established findings in embodied cognition, preconscious processing, affective neuroscience, Bayesian inference, cognitive bias, symbolic compression, and perceptual organization.

They are phenomenological exercises (structured observations of lived experience) grounded in contemporary neuroscience and cognitive science.

## References

Ambady, N., & Rosenthal, R. (1992). Thin slices of expressive behavior as predictors of interpersonal consequences: A meta-analysis. *Psychological Bulletin, 111*(2), 256–274.

Bar, M. (2007). The proactive brain: Using analogies and associations to generate predictions. *Trends in Cognitive Sciences, 11*(7), 280–289.

Barrett, L. F. (2017). *How emotions are made: The secret life of the brain.* Houghton Mifflin Harcourt.

Barrett, L. F., & Simmons, W. K. (2015). Interoceptive predictions in the brain. *Nature Reviews Neuroscience, 16*(7), 419–429.

Bechara, A., Damasio, H., Tranel, D., & Damasio, A. R. (1997). Deciding advantageously before knowing the advantageous strategy. *Science, 275*(5304), 1293–1295.

Blanke, O., & Metzinger, T. (2009). Full-body illusions and minimal phenomenal selfhood. *Trends in Cognitive Sciences, 13*(1), 7–13.

Bowers, K. S., Regehr, G., Balthazard, C., & Parker, K. (1990). Intuition in the context of discovery. *Cognitive Psychology, 22*(1), 72–110.

Cassirer, E. (1944). *An essay on man: An introduction to a philosophy of human culture.* Yale University Press.

Clark, A. (2015). *Surfing uncertainty: Prediction, action, and the embodied mind.* Oxford University Press.

Corbetta, M., & Shulman, G. L. (2002). Control of goal-directed and stimulus-driven attention in the brain. *Nature Reviews Neuroscience, 3*(3), 201–215.

Damasio, A. (1996). The somatic marker hypothesis and the possible functions of the prefrontal cortex. *Philosophical Transactions of the Royal Society B, 351*(1346), 1413–1420.

Damasio, A. (1999). *The feeling of what happens: Body and emotion in the making of consciousness.* Harcourt Brace.

Damasio, A. (2010). *Self comes to mind: Constructing the conscious brain.* Pantheon Books.

Dehaene, S. (2014). *Consciousness and the brain: Deciphering how the brain codes our thoughts.* Viking.

Fleming, S. M., & Dolan, R. J. (2012). The neural basis of metacognitive ability. *Philosophical Transactions of the Royal Society B, 367*(1594), 1338–1349.

Friston, K. (2010). The free-energy principle: A unified brain theory? *Nature Reviews Neuroscience, 11*(2), 127–138.

Friston, K. J., FitzGerald, T., Rigoli, F., Schwartenbeck, P., O'Doherty, J., & Pezzulo, G. (2016). Active inference and learning. *Neuroscience & Biobehavioral Reviews, 68*, 862–879.

Gigerenzer, G. (2007). *Gut feelings: The intelligence of the unconscious.* Viking.

Hohwy, J. (2014). *The predictive mind.* Oxford University Press.

Jung, C. G. (1959). *The archetypes and the collective unconscious* (R. F. C. Hull, Trans.). Princeton University Press.

Jung, C. G. (1964). *Man and his symbols.* Doubleday.

Kahneman, D. (2011). *Thinking, fast and slow.* Farrar, Straus and Giroux.

Kahneman, D., & Klein, G. (2009). Conditions for intuitive expertise: A failure to disagree. *American Psychologist, 64*(6), 515–526.

Kihlstrom, J. F. (1987). The cognitive unconscious. *Science, 237*(4821), 1445–1452.

Kosslyn, S. M. (1994). *Image and brain: The resolution of the imagery debate.* MIT Press.

Lakoff, G., & Johnson, M. (1980). *Metaphors we live by.* University of Chicago Press.

Lakoff, G., & Johnson, M. (1999). *Philosophy in the flesh: The embodied mind and its challenge to Western thought.* Basic Books.

McAdams, D. P. (2001). The psychology of life stories. *Review of General Psychology, 5*(2), 100–122.

Menon, V. (2011). Large-scale brain networks and psychopathology: A unifying triple network model. *Trends in Cognitive Sciences, 15*(10), 483–506.

Merleau-Ponty, M. (2012). *Phenomenology of perception* (D. A. Landes, Trans.). Routledge. (Original work published 1945)

Metzinger, T. (2009). *The ego tunnel: The science of the mind and the myth of the self.* Basic Books.

Nisbett, R. E., & Wilson, T. D. (1977). Telling more than we can know: Verbal reports on mental processes. *Psychological Review, 84*(3), 231–259.

Pearson, J., Naselaris, T., Holmes, E. A., & Kosslyn, S. M. (2015). Mental imagery: Functional mechanisms and clinical applications. *Trends in Cognitive Sciences, 19*(10), 590–602.

Peirce, C. S. (1931–1958). *Collected papers of Charles Sanders Peirce.* Harvard University Press.

Pezzulo, G., Rigoli, F., & Friston, K. (2015). Active inference, homeostatic regulation and adaptive behavioural control. *Cognitive Neuroscience, 6*(4), 187–214.

Ricoeur, P. (1970). *Freud and philosophy: An essay on interpretation.* Yale University Press.

Saussure, F. de (1916). *Course in general linguistics.* McGraw-Hill.

Schacter, D. L., & Addis, D. R. (2007). The cognitive neuroscience of constructive memory: Remembering the past and imagining the future. *Philosophical Transactions of the Royal Society B, 362*(1481), 773–786.

Seeley, W. W., Menon, V., Schatzberg, A. F., Keller, J., Glover, G. H., Kenna, H., Reiss, A. L., & Greicius, M. D. (2007). Dissociable intrinsic connectivity networks for salience processing and executive control. *Journal of Neuroscience, 27*(9), 2349–2356.

Seth, A. (2021). *Being you: A new science of consciousness.* Dutton.

Swann, I. (1991). *Everybody's guide to natural ESP: Unlocking the extrasensory power of your mind.* Jeremy P. Tarcher.

Swann, I. (1993). *Your Nostradamus factor: Accessing your innate ability to see into the future.* Fireside Books.

Swann, I. (1996, February 25). *Remote viewing and signal-to-noise ratio: The "noisy mind/dirty data" issue.* Biomind Superpowers.

Swann, I. (1997, March 1). *Information, information theory and information transfer.* Biomind Superpowers.

Swann, I. (1998, November 16). *The superpower faculties vs. maps of the mind.* Biomind Superpowers.

Swann, I. (2018). *Psychic Literacy: & the Coming Psychic Renaissance.* Swann-Ryder Productions.

Swann, I. (n.d.). *Loose diagrams* [Unpublished materials]. Ingo Swann Papers, Special Collections, Irvine S. Ingram Library, University of West Georgia.

Thompson, E. (2007). *Mind in life: Biology, phenomenology, and the sciences of mind.* Harvard University Press.

Tversky, A., & Kahneman, D. (1974). Judgment under uncertainty: Heuristics and biases. *Science, 185*(4157), 1124–1131.

# THE SERIES
## You Are More Than You Think

**Book One**
What's Already There

**Book Two**
Where You Sit

**Book Three**
The Shape of Knowing

**Book Four**
Above the Noise

**Book Five**
The Gravity of Reality

Chapter numbers continue across volumes to reflect that the series unfolds as one integrated structure rather than as separate works. Each book stands on its own, but the numbering maintains the progression for readers who move across the entire sequence.

Elly Flippen is the niece of Ingo Swann and the editor of **Why Do We Feel There Is More to Us Than We, or Anyone, Knows About?**, as well as the author of **Conjunction.World.**

Her work is shaped by years of engagement with questions of perception, awareness, and the lived experience of human intelligence beyond habit and assumption.

She invites readers to rely on their own sensing and discernment, recognizing perception not as something to acquire, but as something already active and waiting to be understood.

To learn more about Ingo Swann and his work, visit **www.ingoswann.com.**